BEYOND ME:

A Christ-Centered
Approach to Self-Esteem

Beyond me

NORMA KVINDLOG and
ESTHER LINDGREN ANDERSON

Tyndale House Publishers, Inc.
Wheaton, Illinois

ACKNOWLEDGMENTS

We are grateful to the many who have helped make this book a reality:

- those we have been privileged to teach and who in turn have taught us so much;
- Jan Kleeman, who insisted we write our teachings in book form;
- our pastor, Jim Danhof, for his continual encouragement;
- Ruth Clemmons, for her wise and loving help in editing and the many hours she cheerfully gave to that task;
- Terri Hungerford and Nancy Maehl for willingly— even eagerly—typing our first draft;
- Jeanne Cargin, who used her inquiring mind to help write provocative questions;
- Dawn Sundquist, our sweet-spirited editor whom we love as a daughter and respect as a mentor;
- our children, who were unwittingly our guinea pigs long before we had ever heard the term *self-esteem;*
- and especially our loving, supportive husbands, who never complained of neglect but pitched in to help with daily responsibilities, freeing us to write.

What began as a class for mothers in Vacation Bible School has stretched into an exciting eight-year adventure. We thank God for putting us together to teach and write. We marvel repeatedly at the truths that surface as we share totally differing experiences with that two-sided coin, pride.

Each of us is grateful for the enriching perspective the other brought to our work. Twenty years of friendship and service together has built a strong foundation of love, respect, and unity that has weathered the difficulties of writing and enhanced its exciting aspects. We say "Amen" to the truth of Ecclesiastes 4:9:

Two are better than one, because they have a good (more satisfying) reward for their labor. (Amp)

The stories and illustrations in this book are based on actual experiences. However, the names of the persons involved have been changed to protect their identities.

Bible verses are quoted from *The Amplified Bible* (Amp) © 1965 by Zondervan Publishing House, Grand Rapids, Michigan; *The Holy Bible,* New International Version (NIV) © 1978 by the New York International Bible Society, used by permission of Zondervan Bible Publishers; *The Living Bible* (TLB) © 1971 by Tyndale House Publishers, Wheaton, Illinois; *The New American Standard Bible* (NASB) © 1960, 1962, 1963, 1968, 1971, 1972, 1973, 1975, 1977 by the Lockman Foundation, La Habra, California.

First printing, April 1987
Library of Congress Catalog Card Number 87-50008
ISBN 0-8423-1310-9
© 1987 by Norma Kvindlog and Esther Lindgren Anderson
Printed in the United States of America

To our husbands, Don and Jim,
and our children—
David and Leanne
Sue, Steve, Laurel, and Holli

CONTENTS

PREFACE

More than ninety adolescents have passed through my home in the past twenty years. Though their stays ranged from one month to six years, they all had one thing in common: They didn't like themselves very much. Most adolescents don't. But even among adults today, insecurity and self-hatred seem to be the name of the game.

The consequences of not feeling good about oneself are always unhappy—and sometimes tragic. A lack of self-acceptance has shaped Ginny into a fearful, withdrawn adult, Ted into an overbearing attention-seeker, and Molly into a defiant, promiscuous nonconformist. It has caused Andrea to cry with anguish, "My own parents don't like me and I can't stand myself, so how can God love me?"

Working closely with young people and their families as a foster mother has underscored for me the deep self-esteem needs of every person, regardless of age. This shared aware-ness prompted Norma Kvindlog and me to develop a course on instilling biblical, healthy self-esteem in ourselves and others. In each of the forty-plus times we presented it, we were we are asked to write it down. This book is our response.

Our book reflects the story of a pilgrimage. We offer

these insights not because we have arrived, but because we hope others will be helped by what we have learned along the way. Many times we leave our class convicted by the truth God has revealed to us even while we are teaching. Sometimes we feel brokenhearted over the mistakes we suddenly see so clearly in our child-raising and in our other relationships. Like all parents of grown children, we have some deep regrets.

But as we teach others and learn ourselves, we see lives changed through the development of godly self-esteem. We know of relationships healed and enhanced. Blessings come from using biblical teachings to recognize our position in Christ, our value to him, and our potential through him. Wrote Kim, one participant:

Rarely did I allow others to know how unsure I was of myself. After the second session [of your class] I forced myself to look at my assets. I don't know just when I realized I liked myself. Someplace inside of me a button switched from peer acceptance to self-acceptance. Our family has reaped benefits because I am consciously trying to reinforce the positive traits that build healthy self-esteem.

Once we discover God's cure for unhealthy self-esteem we can spread it to others, and those we love will be the first to benefit. We can give our families a place of refuge where each individual is respected and given a sense of worth. We won't have to cave in to selfishness, protecting our own egos at the expense of others.

Jody, a Christian musician, is one of those who discovered new ways to relate to her family. She had found "acceptance" in the world of hard rock and hard drugs before turning her life over to Christ and experiencing his unconditional love. Today she writes:

Through your course I learned specific and practical ways to alter my thought patterns. . . . It was also very reassuring to me to discover that low self-esteem is suffered by everyone at some point in life. . . . Perhaps most important, I learned how I can avoid passing on the tendency for low self-esteem to my children.

[Recently] we played at a huge youth convention. . . . I shared my story and people spoke to me afterward, begging for something they could read or do to help themselves. Too bad they weren't here to take your class! People identify with my low self-esteem problems everywhere we play and minister. Satan is really doing a job of confusing us all!

In time, our growing self-esteem will benefit all those whose lives touch ours. We were delighted to learn that Margaret, a withdrawn senior citizen who had never said a word throughout the sessions, has begun to teach a Sunday school class of her peers and is showing a special sensitivity to its needs. She said, "I followed your steps to good self-esteem. I am even learning to recognize poor self-esteem in other people, and now I know how to help them!"

Perhaps the greatest benefit of a healthy self-esteem is an enhanced relationship with Christ. One pastor, writing to thank us for speaking to his congregation, added this comment: "I am convinced that very few people really have the proper foundation for these concepts, and that is one of the tragedies of the church today." His response was confirmed by a reader of *Discipleship Journal,* who wrote to its editor:

One of the prerequisites to living a life of obedience is an adequate self-concept. Changing an inadequate self-concept is very difficult but often very necessary. We need material that deals with this aspect of disciple-making.

We hope what follows will meet that need—and help you and your family enjoy all the benefits of a truly healthy self-esteem.

Esther Lindgren Anderson

Part One

identifying unhealthy self-esteem

1 What's Healthy?
The Two Faces of Pride

Ellie hung up the phone, feeling depressed again, and reached for the package of Twinkies she had hidden behind the cake flour.

"She didn't even thank me for giving Brian a ride to gym class. I don't think Marcie realizes how many times I've taken him. All she can talk about is how well he does at the meets and how much they work with him.

"Well, Fred and I are just not as athletic as she and Norman. And we don't have all that time to work with Robbie. Even if we did, he'd never try as hard as Brian does anyway.

"Why does everything they do turn out so right? Why can't we ever do anything as well? If only Fred were like Norman, maybe our lives would be better, too!"

A COMMON MALADY

Ellie may not know it, but she has a case of unhealthy self-esteem.

Unhealthy self-esteem is simply a product of an overconcern with *self*. Many people today struggle with it. Answer the questions below to see if you have any of the symptoms.

- Do I feel threatened by the success of others?
- Do I think others often put me down?
- Do I frequently feel nobody likes or appreciates me?
- Does criticism infuriate me, or always seem unjustified and unfair?
- Do I need a lot of praise to feel secure?
- Do I have a critical attitude toward myself?

If you answered yes to one or more of these questions, you, too, may be infected with a case of unhealthy self-esteem.

Where does unhealthy self-esteem start? How does it make such headway? And how can we turn it around?

THE WRONG DIAGNOSIS

Self-esteem therapy, which is very popular today, often promotes an emphasis on self. Many people are being told, in effect, "You are the most important person in your life, and what you want for yourself is more important than what anyone else wants for you."

This approach may be helpful to the oppressed person or to the one who is being pressured into inappropriate behavior by his peer group. But unfortunately, we hear what we want to hear. Young people tend to take this counsel as a license to defy authority in their lives. Others use it as an excuse to play down and even disregard the rights and the needs of others. So this view of self-esteem tends to be counterproductive. Putting oneself first is neither healthy nor biblical!

To find the real cure for unhealthy self-esteem, we must first understand its source: pride.

WHERE UNHEALTHY SELF-ESTEEM STARTS

Pride is like a two-sided coin. It can manifest itself in feelings of inferiority or in feelings of superiority.

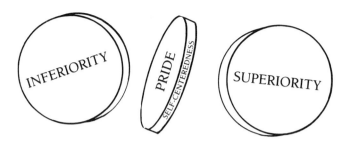

We readily recognize the pride inherent in a sense of superiority, but we fail to see that inferiority also promotes a self-focus. And that self-focus is the root of pride and its offshoot, unhealthy self-esteem.

Our friend, Ellie, for example, was wallowing in a pool of self-pity. She felt inferior to Marcie. But her pity party degenerated into resentful feelings toward her friend. Anger, criticism, and faultfinding are as much expressions of unhealthy self-esteem as self-pity. The leap from inferiority to superiority represents the whole spectrum of unhealthy self-esteem.

Pride is like a bouncing ball:
"Sometimes I'm up, sometimes I'm down. . . ."

Tragically, pride feeds itself through comparisons with others. A person with an unhealthy self-esteem will ask himself, "Am I attractive enough? Smart enough? Loved enough? Do other people treat me right?" At other times, his ego may whisper, "See? I am brighter . . . more attractive . . . more successful than other people." Either way, the bottom-line question in his mind is "How do I compare with others? How do I stack up against the competition?"

If only we could feel like equals instead of rivals! If only we could see ourselves and others realistically, each with some good points and some not-so-good points! That will happen when we begin to grow in our understanding of healthy self-esteem.

THE REAL MEANING OF HUMILITY

Unhealthy self-esteem has often been confused with humility. But true humility grows out of an appraisal of one's self that doesn't depend on comparisons—positive or negative—with others.

As C. S. Lewis says, humility is not the same as having a low opinion of your talents and character, nor is it claiming that your talent is less valuable than you know it to be. Humility is simply self-forgetfulness.[1]

Do not imagine that if you meet a really humble man he will be what most people call "humble" nowadays. . . . Probably all you will think about him is that he seemed a cheerful, intelligent chap who took a real interest in what you said to him. If you do dislike him it will be because you will feel a little envious of anyone who seems to enjoy life so easily. He will not be thinking about humility; he will not be thinking about himself at all.[2]

Did Jesus exhibit low self-esteem in the classic passage on his humility in Philippians 2? Obviously not! He knew who he was. He understood his position, his value, and his relationship to the Father. Yet he is given as our example. He was the epitome of selflessness, and only through him can we begin to move from self-preoccupation to self-forgetfulness. We will discuss this process more in later chapters.

CRIPPLING EFFECTS OF LOW SELF-ESTEEM

The malady of unhealthy self-esteem cripples us emotionally in many ways. For instance, low self-esteem hinders us from showing concern for others. How can you reach out to lonely, hurting people when you're focused on yourself? If you feel inadequate, you will hold yourself apart from others for fear of rejection. It's easier to stay at home than to go to a social gathering alone. ("Everyone else will be with

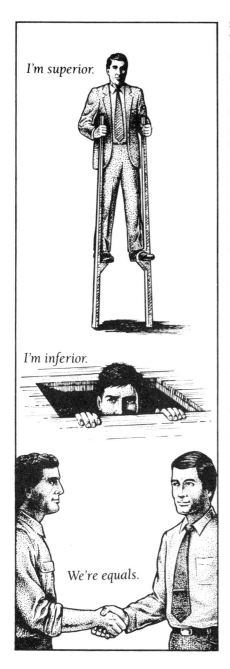

I'm superior.

I'm inferior.

We're equals.

someone," you think.) You put off phoning the one going through a crisis. ("She must be tired of everyone calling.") You never get around to having that group of people over. ("They're probably busy with other friends.") And you think someone else will speak to the stranger at church. ("Others find that easier to do.")

Unhealthy self-esteem can also cause us to see the worst in others. If a sense of inadequacy doesn't throw up a wall, a judgmental attitude will. We may not recognize our feelings of superiority, but our tone of voice and body language can unconsciously convey a cold message: "You are inferior to me." Even in instances when our criticism is justified, we may be voicing it because we feel superior or because we *need* to feel superior to someone else in order to feel good about ourselves. If, as with Ellie, our feelings of inferiority become intense, subconsciously we may begin to *look* for something to criticize in someone else.

Low self-esteem can also make us feel dissatisfied with ourselves. Feelings of inferiority rob you of joy and confidence. But a superior attitude can also tear you down if your self-expectations become unrealistic or unattainable. With either attitude, how can you measure up to the ideal? Either way, how can you be satisfied with your role in life?

SIDE-EFFECTS OF HEALTHY SELF-ESTEEM

We asked a group of people the question, "How do you know when your self-esteem is healthy?" Their discussion reinforced some basic points:

- When you feel confident
- When you can admit you need to change and grow
- When you are willing to change
- When you can accept others as they are
- When you can correct self-centered thought patterns
- When you believe God loves you as you are

If Ellie, for example, had healthy self-esteem, she wouldn't feel so threatened by the abilities and successes of Marcie's family. She would better accept her husband's shortcomings. And she would be more open and honest in all her relationships instead of allowing secret resentments to fester.

Why suffer with a set of unhealthy responses like Ellie's when you can choose to change? A good dose of healthy self-esteem would free us all from destructive comparison and allow us to experience more godly love and concern for others.

So take the first step away from the two faces of pride toward healthy self-esteem. Determine to change.

QUESTIONS FOR PERSONAL APPLICATION

1. Which symptoms of unhealthy self-esteem are most often yours?
2. Which face of pride best describes you?
3. Think of someone of whom you are critical. Is it because you feel inferior to that person? Or because you feel superior?
4. Do you subconsciously decide whether you are better than or inferior to the people you meet?
5. In what ways do your feelings of inadequacy keep you from reaching out to others?
6. What do you sometimes say or do that may cause others to feel inferior to you? How might your attitude convey superiority?
7. What signs of a healthy self-esteem (page 22) do you need to work on as you read this book?
8. What specific self-centered attitudes or actions do you need to confess to God as pride?
9. In what ways can you be more understanding and accepting of what you see as shortcomings in your husband or wife?

   In your children?
   In your friends?
   In your parents and other family members?
   In your coworkers?
   In your pastor?

   Remember, other people see traits in you that they don't like either. The next time you are tempted to be critical of the shortcomings of others, instead thank God for any acceptance others have given you in spite of *your* inadequacies.
10. Answer questions 7 and 8 from the questions below.

QUESTIONS FOR GROUP DISCUSSION

1. As a group, make up your own list of symptoms of unhealthy self-esteem. Then list the qualities you think exemplify healthy self-esteem.
2. Can you think of circumstances or types of people that tempt you to become critical? What kinds of people or circumstances cause you to feel inferior?
3. How can a person have feelings of inferiority and superiority at the same time?
4. How can you tell whether a person's overbearing attitude is due to a sense of inferiority or to a sense of superiority?
5. Discuss the difference between low self-esteem and humility. How is low self-esteem related to pride?
6. How does C. S. Lewis's definition of humility differ from other definitions you have heard?

7. Can you think of times when feelings of inadequacy would keep people from being sociable or reaching out to others? What are some of the excuses given to justify such behavior?

8. What do you learn about humility from Romans 12:3; Philippians 3:7-14; 4:11-13; 1 Peter 5:5-7?

9. Discuss the true humility of Jesus as described in Philippians 2:3-11. How can we apply his example to our own lives? What else do you learn about humility from Jesus' life on earth as recorded in the Gospels?

2 Be Careful, It's Contagious!
How Unhealthy Attitudes Spread

I really hated myself when I was in high school, and maybe that's why I hated my parents, too. They compared me unfavorably with other kids, and I felt that no matter what I did, I couldn't please them. We were ugly to each other. Do you suppose that was because none of us liked ourselves?

Our young friend is right on target! We all exert a remarkable influence on the self-esteem of others. Your parents, or the ones who raised you, were the most important people in your life as a child, so the way they reacted to you strongly influenced your self-image. Let's take that thought a step further:

- The way parents feel about themselves affects how they respond to their child.
- The way parents respond to their child affects how the child feels about himself.
- The way a child feels about himself affects how he responds to his parents.
- The way a child responds to his parents affects how the parents feel about themselves.

It's a full circle!

Because of the effect we have on one another, a husband and father who accepts himself can create an atmosphere of mutual respect and enjoyment at home. His family can feel pleasure at his homecoming because he reacts with pleasure toward them. He doesn't put on a false happy face and try to hide all the hurts and frustrations of the day, but he does communicate, "I'm glad to be with you again."

Warm, accepting behavior is reciprocal. The mutual appreciation of husband and wife builds on itself and spills over onto the children.

Does such a couple ever disagree? Sure they do! Do they ever get angry? Of course. But the disagreement is handled in that same atmosphere of mutual respect, which doesn't need a scapegoat and doesn't find satisfaction in tearing down the other person.

REJECTION IN THE HOME

Rejecting behavior is reciprocal, too. It's a little unnerving to realize that a poor attitude can so easily be transferred from mate to mate and from parent to child! Where do destructive attitudes come from, and how are they passed on?

If you cope with unhealthy self-esteem through a predominantly superior attitude, your focus on self is often transferred to your children through critical put-downs. (You might try to excuse yourself in the name of helping them to be more acceptable.)

The American Institute of Family Relations cites a survey in which parents were asked to record how many negative— as opposed to positive—comments they made to their children. The findings: Parents criticize their children ten times for every one time they make a favorable comment.

Even without confrontation, you can pass on your critical attitude through nonverbal communication or your criticism of others.

If your response to unhealthy self-esteem follows a pattern of inferiority, you may not criticize openly—or even indirectly. Perhaps you simply withdraw from esteem-threatening situations for fear of rejection. Over time, your behavior can lead to a sense of social inadequacy, and that lack of self-confidence in and out of the home is passed on to the family. Parental passivity is one problem-causing result of poor self-esteem.

When a parent is passive, he often fails to correct his children, even though he may support them in every other way. The result is an unhealthy emotional climate.

- Failure to lay out and enforce clear guidelines allows a child's unacceptable behavior to continue unchecked; his unpleasant traits will result in rejection as an adult.
- Failure to provide protective limits forces a child to take responsibility for his behavior before he is equipped to handle it, adding to his feelings of self-doubt.
- Failure to enforce respectful behavior within the home allows sibling rivalry to turn into verbal—and even physical—free-for-alls that may inflict lasting injury to a child's self-worth.

Ultimately, your self-esteem affects not only how you handle your children, but how they come to see themselves and other people.

A BAD DAY'S MESSAGE

Remember this scenario? You came home from school nursing a wound inflicted by a critical classmate or teacher, only to find yourself the target of your mother's bad mood; she had felt slighted by a friend that day and was transferring the hurt to you.

Then Dad came home, uncommunicative and short-tempered, venting his frustration on the family because he hadn't received the recognition he felt he deserved at work—or worse, his boss had put him down in front of others.

Your siblings bickered among themselves.

The scene was set for an evening of angry fighting or hostile silence, depending on your family's method of coping. Either way, the message came across loud and clear to each of you from the others: "I don't like the way you are!"

But lest we blame our parents for all of our problems, we need to remember they received imperfect parenting, too. And you will parent just as you were parented, say psychologists, unless you make some deliberate changes in your attitudes and techniques. Even then, you may unwittingly pass on some measure of unhealthy self-esteem to your children.

A reader shared the following letter with Ann Landers:

Dear Ann: I have read so many letters in your column from children and adults who blame their parents for raising them "wrong." They complain because they are high-strung and unmotivated.

Why don't these people understand that their parents had parents, too? If a person is going to lay all his problems on his parents' backs, he must also blame his grandparents and his great-grandparents.

Raising children is the hardest job there is. It's one job for which there can be no previous training. I was mad at my parents for years because I felt unloved. Now I know they couldn't help being the way they were. But I did change some things about myself I didn't like when I realized blaming them solved no problems. It only made me bitter.

I won't be a perfect parent by a long shot, but I hope my children will forgive me for my inadequacies. I guess one has to become a parent before he can forgive his own.
(Signed) It Happened to Me

REJECTION OUTSIDE THE HOME

Even for those who receive positive parenting, blows to the
ego may still be a significant part of life away from home—
sometimes excruciatingly so. Karen told us a story that
makes us weep inside:

*I was shy and quiet, one of the anonymous faces in school, and
I had never had a regular date. So I was overwhelmed when
one of the most popular boys in my class asked me to the prom.*

*I worked extra hours for money to buy material for my
dream dress, and I also made a dress for my younger sister,
who had a steady boyfriend.*

*By prom night I was almost sick with anticipation. My
sister's date arrived, and we sat in uncomfortable silence,
waiting. And waiting. And waiting. Finally my sister's date
confessed that it had all been a joke; my "date" had never
intended to escort me to the prom. He had had another date
from the beginning. Going back to school the next week was
one of the hardest things I have ever had to do.*

That kind of anguish can never be expressed in words.
Even decades later the painful details can still be recalled,
the hurt and humiliation still felt.

Perhaps the severity of Karen's trauma is unusual, but
none of us entirely escapes the blows to our self-esteem that
originate outside the home. We all experience some type of
rejection and put-downs as we are growing up, and our
developing personalities are strongly influenced by these
experiences. We try to collect clues from other people all
along the way as to how acceptable, how lovable, we are to
them. So, to the influence of home life, we must add the
imprint made on our self-esteem by teachers, other adults,
and peers.

It is easy to see why the feelings you carried into adoles-
cence could have been those of inadequacy and deep dis-
satisfaction with yourself. If those feelings continue into

adulthood, they will hurt all of your relationships. As with your family interaction in childhood: how you feel about yourself affects how you react to others,

. . . which affects how they feel about themselves,
. . . which affects how they react to you,
. . . which affects how you feel about yourself.

It's a full circle again.

BREAKING THE CYCLE

Unhealthy self-esteem is highly contagious, but it needn't be crippling. It is never too late to heal the damage inflicted by past relationships.

What good does it do to cling to old resentments? Is there any benefit in remembering past injury? Why should a rejection during the unstable teen years affect your self-worth now? Or a slight last year, or last month, or last week? You need to forgive anyone who has ever hurt you, including your parents. This is an important lesson: *forgiveness is the beginning of healthy self-esteem.*

If you can enjoy who you are, your happy attitude will make your own imperfections less important—and my imperfections will seem less important, too! You'll be able to help me feel good about myself because of your uncritical attitude toward yourself and toward me. You can reach out in friendship, knowing that everyone needs more strokes, and not feel slighted if someone doesn't seem to accept your friendly gestures. You won't allow your self-protectiveness to blind you to my real needs. As a result, your self-acceptance can help build mine, and I'll be able to say, "Talking with you makes me feel so much better!"

Healthy self-esteem can be just as contagious as the unhealthy variety. Let's turn the negative to the positive:

Because I like the way I am,
I can like the way you are,
and help you like yourself!

QUESTIONS FOR PERSONAL APPLICATION

1. In what ways do you think your parents shaped your self-image positively? Negatively? In what ways did your parents' self-esteem reveal itself?
2. What other strong influences on your self-worth do you remember from childhood? Be specific; cite instances. Consider your teachers, your siblings, your peers, and humiliating or encouraging incidents.
3. Do you harbor grudges? Or does your attitude show you have forgiven those who have hurt you?
4. Are you passing on healthy or unhealthy self-esteem? Is your unhealthy self-esteem revealed mostly through critical put-downs? Or through silence and withdrawal? In other ways?
5. Are some of your parenting techniques identical to your parents'? Are the methods desirable? If not, what will you do to change?
6. Keep a record of your critical and favorable comments to your children for a day. How do you compare with the survey?
7. What ways can you help offset your negative comments with positive input?
8. What imperfections make you critical of yourself? Do you find yourself being critical of others for those same faults?
9. Think of someone close to you who needs a boost. Plan what you can do or say to meet that need.

QUESTIONS FOR GROUP DISCUSSION

1. Discuss some specific ways an unhealthy self-image might manifest itself in a parent and his child. Follow each example the full circle—from parent to child and back to the parent.
2. How does a superior attitude show itself nonverbally in a person's behavior? An inferior attitude?
3. Which adults in your growing-up years helped you to have a positive self-image? How can you be more like them?
4. Discuss how husbands and wives can show understanding of each others' special esteem needs at the end of the workday.
5. What are some of the ways children mask the hurts and difficulties they experience at school and play? Why do they try to hide their problems? How can parents help?
6. Select prayer partners for this week to pray that family members might become more aware of each others' esteem needs.

3   I'm a Carrier
Making Communication Count

It's snapshot time. The group mills around, each person jockeying for position. Suddenly cousin Susie squeals, "Ooh, wait, let me get behind you; I don't want to be in front!"

Do you stand partly behind someone else for a family snapshot? Do you allow only your good side to be photographed? When group pictures are developed, do you look for your own image first.

If you're like most people, your answers are yes. Self-esteem is affected by the way we think we appear to others, and pictures can be reassuring—or more than we wish, painful reminders of visible inadequacies.

WHAT'S YOUR SELF-IMAGE?

Self-esteem: the value you place on yourself
+ Self-image: the picture you have of yourself
= Self-concept: the total idea you have of yourself

The value you place on yourself (self-esteem) rests on the picture you have of yourself (self-image). Self-image is made up of many facets, including:

- physical appearance,
- intelligence,
- personality,
- socioeconomic status,
- talents and abilities,
- roles in life,
- beliefs, attitudes, and values.

(We will discuss the first four facets in chapters 4–7.)

As you view each facet of yourself, a distinct picture begins to emerge. Let's take your appearance, for example. First and foremost, are you too fat or too flat, too flabby or too bony? Do you like the shape of your face, your nose, your mouth? How's your complexion? Is your hair too curly, too straight, too sparse, too gray? Anything else wrong? Right?

Do you magnify your imperfections? Why are you so critical of yourself? Where do your standards come from?

Most often we compare ourselves to ideals we learn from other people. From television, movies, and advertising. From the critical judgments our friends apply to others. Too often self-image is not so much the way we see ourselves as it is *the way we think others see us.*

Each facet of your self-image is acquired in the same way—from others. When it comes to your view of your intelligence, school experiences can be devastating—or exhilarating. Either way, they are remembered for a lifetime. Even the most casual attitudes and comments linger in your memory, don't they?

In every facet of our self-image, what we believe others think of us determines the value we place on ourselves. We subconsciously score ourselves according to how highly we value their judgment. Meanwhile they are doing the same.

Always, inwardly, each one of us is crying out, "Please tell me I'm OK!"

WHY OTHER PEOPLE AREN'T ALWAYS RIGHT

We are so easily lifted up or knocked down by the opinions others have of us. We rise or fall depending on whether they commend, criticize, reward, or ignore us. But the actions of other people are influenced by a number of factors:

- their self-esteem,
- their understanding,
- their background,

none of which is ever fully communicated. To add to the confusion, their input is evaluated by you according to:

- your self-esteem,
- your understanding,
- your background.

So we can well agree, "I know you believe you understand what you think I said, but I'm not sure you realize that what you heard is not what I meant."

No wonder there is so much breakdown in human communication! When two people talk or write to each other, there are actually eight personalities present:

1. You
2. Me
3. Who I think I am
4. Who you think you are
5. Who you think I am
6. Who I think you are
7. Who I think you think you are
8. Who you think I think I am

Your friend may intend nothing derogatory by a remark he or she makes to you, but if you are feeling down for any reason, it can become another blow to your ego.

When a friend to whom I already felt inferior came to my home and said (meaning to be helpful), "This room would look larger if you'd paint it a lighter color," and added, "You need a big plant in that corner," I knew I couldn't measure up to her standards. I felt my house wasn't good enough for her, my husband wasn't as good a provider as hers, and I was an inadequate homemaker and decorator.

Any time someone to whom you already feel inferior offers unsolicited advice, your self-worth takes another nose dive. Ever notice how much easier it is to take advice from someone who doesn't seem superior to you? Perhaps this is why adolescents accept advice so much more readily from peers than from parents.

If you feel inadequate in any area—

- in your parenting,
- in your homemaking,
- in your job,
- in your marriage,
- in your other relationships—

you will tend to respond with supersensitivity to negative input in that area. If your sense of inadequacy is severe, you may react strongly to criticism in other areas as well.

You end up hurting other people when you hurt inside. For example, you may lash out at your child because you feel inadequate in your parenting skills or in another family relationship. Physical problems—or simple weariness—can also create a defensive attitude, misunderstandings, and needless hurt.

Our resident boarder was taking each piece of her ironing from the dining room to the hall closet as she finished it. I suggested she could do as I usually did—hang the ironed clothes from the dining room chandelier instead. She stepped back, looked up critically at the chandelier, and said, "Well, it looks dirty." But she proceeded to do as I suggested.

I was already having problems with guilt over my inability to keep up with the housework (because of physical problems), so her blunt criticism was a real blow. I said nothing, but inwardly I seethed, both at her and at myself. Hours later I was still feeling the sting when suddenly a light bulb went on in my head. "Well, it looks sturdy," is what she had actually said! I never told her how I had misunderstood.

Even when others are trying to build us up, we can misread both their words and their intent when our self-esteem is lacking.

One of our foster daughter's early years had left deep scars, and she felt hostile toward the world. She was convinced others were always putting her down. I tried to make her feel better by suggesting that she may have misunderstood the meaning of the words and actions she felt were directed against her; perhaps no malice had been involved. Then one day I chanced to overhear how she had been taking my intended comfort: "Mom always assumes I'm wrong; she always takes the other guy's side against me!"

Interaction with others *cannot* give us an accurate evaluation of our self-worth, yet it remains our main, and often only, source of reference.

THE POWER OF LABELS

If we could see how strongly our communication with others affects their self-worth, we might be more careful of the messages we send. We wouldn't be so quick to label others negatively. We especially would watch what we say about children who are too easily labeled as:

- troublemakers,
- stupid,
- slow,

- lazy,
- disobedient,
- scatterbrained.

These labels often become self-fulfilling prophecies, as many experiments verify.

But the good news is that labels work positively, too. In one experiment, teachers were told that a group of children, selected randomly from the class, had scored high on a test for "intellectual blooming." Actually, their scores were no different from those of the others in the class. But the teachers *believed* those children had a high potential for intellectual growth, and mentally labeled them accordingly. Apparently the students sensed their teacher's attitude, because they lived up to those expectations.[1]

We tend to become not only what others think we are but what *we* think we are. "For as he thinks within himself, so he is" (Prov. 23:7, NASB).

Some of our traits might be the product of someone's propaganda. "You'd forget your head if it weren't screwed on," or "I have a memory like a sieve, and you're just like me." "You're as clumsy as your father," or "We're both klutzes, aren't we?"

Says one therapist, "The traits parents choose to comment upon or assign can be retained into adult life as part of a person's self-definition." Another quotes a forgetful woman: "Ever since I was a child I've been called a sweet little scatterbrain, so maybe I've just learned to fulfill everyone's expectations."[2]

"One of the surest ways to keep messing up is to anticipate that you will," say therapists.

People who put themselves down develop a predisposition for not doing well because they're not seeing themselves as capable individuals. . . . There is a common tendency among people who berate themselves unnecessarily to believe in the myth of

*the perfect person, and to see themselves as inadequate by
contrast. It's very intimidating to feel everybody else knows
how to do things right.*

You don't need to keep replaying the negative tapes in
your memory. You *can* change your self-image by dropping
bad labels about yourself. Instead of thinking, "That was a
stupid thing to do; I must be a stupid person," tell yourself,
"I may have done something foolish, but that doesn't make
me stupid."

- If you consider yourself capable, you will perform more
  adequately.
- If you think you are liked by others, you will be able to
  reach out to them.
- If you feel attractive, your personality can make you so,
  even though your features may be far from perfect.

But perhaps that seems too simplistic to you, a Polly-
annish solution to an impossible situation. Perhaps those
negative labels are so much a part of you that you feel stuck
with them. Even though you know they undermine your
self-confidence, you feel incapable of change.

Sandy felt rejected as a child, held outside the family
circle. She was made to feel unacceptable. Although she is
now a wife and mother, she is still lonely, withdrawn, and
afraid of people outside her home. Her parenting is inevita-
bly affected also; she is too fearful to adequately nurture her
child.

When we suggested that one way she could develop a
positive attitude toward herself would be to show concern
for others, she wrote:

*Your advice sounds solid and good. However, at this point I am
not able to do the things you suggest. I am probably one of the
most fearful people you have known. I am so afraid of every-
thing that I am immobilized by it. I want to change my life,*

but I can't do it alone. My husband can't help me as he, too, is afraid of developing relationships with people.

Sandy's right. She can't do it alone, and help from her husband isn't the answer. Change has to come from within a person through his or her relationship with God. God can give us the ability to change, but we need to utilize the power he promises, the strength he offers.

Why do we fail to draw upon his strength? Because it isn't easy to believe he will provide what we need. It isn't easy to walk by faith. But when we do trust him, we free him to do his discipling work in our lives and to reflect his character in us day by day.

When you start to believe that God will do what he says he will do for you, you'll take the first step toward overcoming the negative communication you have experienced. Eventually you'll be able to:

- forgive those who brought it,
- discount most of it as invalid,
- evaluate yourself more realistically.

SILENCE NEGATIVE VOICES!

How can you look at yourself realistically? What practical steps can you take to change negative attitudes toward yourself?

1. Make a list of the areas in which you *know* yourself to be competent. Put facts before feelings as you look at your abilities. Then say to yourself, "I *do* have some good qualities; I *am* an able person in some areas." Heed the old song and "accentuate the positive, eliminate the negative, latch onto the affirmative!"

2. Try to see that other people have needs and hurts just as you do, no matter how together they seem to be. Then focus on how you might help to meet those needs rather than on how other people need to meet yours.

3. If there are some things about you that others don't

seem to like, try not to respond defensively. Instead, see the criticism as a possible help in your life. Consider whether there are some changes you need to make.

4. Accept yourself as you are—imperfections and all. Thank God for your uniqueness and the uniquenesses of others.

5. Pray with St. Francis of Assisi, "God grant me the serenity to accept the things I cannot change, the courage to change the things I can, and the wisdom to know the difference." You can't change your height or the size of your feet or the circumstances of your birth. But with the help of God you *can* change your attitude toward them.

Imagine what could happen in your life if you would begin to look positively at yourself! Then you could pass on to others the feeling that they are OK, too. What a boost to your family and friends—and even to yourself—if you would communicate that you believe in the high potential of each of them, you accept their uniqueness, and you respect who each one is right now.

You are a carrier, so pass along the positive. I'm very susceptible, so please tell me I'm OK!

QUESTIONS FOR PERSONAL APPLICATION

1. Do you tend to place too much value on others' opinions of you?
2. How do you react when someone seems to be criticizing you? Try to think whether you could be misinterpreting the intent. How can you more fairly evaluate such input?
3. Has labeling affected your life? Which labels have you lived up to? Which labels have you attached to someone else? If they were negative labels, how can you break the patterns they have made in your life or in another's?
4. What can you say to each family member today to communicate your belief in him, your acceptance of him, and your respect for him?
5. Can you think of instances where people have given you unsolicited advice? How did you feel? How did you respond? Did your previous attitude toward that person affect your response?
6. Have you withheld help or encouragement from someone because you do not feel equal to him? How can you change your attitude?
7. In what areas of your life do you feel inadequate? List your good

qualities and areas of competency. Thank God for them and consider how you could better use them for his glory.

8. List the things you don't like about yourself. Circle those that cannot be changed. Ask God for the serenity to accept them. Star the things that God would want you to change. Ask him for the will to start making changes.

QUESTIONS FOR GROUP DISCUSSION

1. Name some of the ungodly standards with which we have been subtly brainwashed. Consider TV and movies, advertising, peers, and your school system.

2. Do you care more about measuring up to the expectations of family members or to those of a casual acquaintance? What would determine your answer to this?

3. How might the way you feel about yourself at the moment affect how you perceive what is said about you? Consider how differently you would react to a statement right after you had received a pat on the back and after you had been criticized.

4. From what kinds of people is it hard to accept advice? Why?

5. From your childhood, recall an adult who seemed to think you had potential. What effect did that have on you?

6. Recall an adult who gave you a negative or positive label. Are you still carrying that label?

7. As a group, share promises from God's Word that you can claim in order to encourage positive attitudes.

8. What concept in the first three chapters has challenged you the most? Why?

9. What area would you most like to see changed in your own life and in your family life? Select prayer partners to pray about these requests this week.

4 I'm Susceptible: How Do I Look?
Your Body Image and Self-Esteem

To paraphrase Abraham Lincoln, God must love ordinary-looking people because he made so many of them. But for most of us, looking ordinary isn't good enough. How many of us can say we like the way we look?

IDEALIZED LOOKS

During my adolescence I devoured the Christian novels of Grace Livingston Hill and the western romances of William McLeod Raine and Zane Grey. In everything I read or heard, the message came through loud and clear: Worthwhile men are tall, handsome, athletic, and rich. Truly admirable women are beautiful and petite, with small, slender hands and feet and impeccable taste in clothes.

Many fiction writers seem to have a peculiar preoccupation with a character's face and body image. Even children very quickly understand that beauty equals goodness and kindness and nobility, while ugliness equals badness and meanness and unscrupulous behavior. Large, wide-set eyes denote gentle innocence, but people with small, close-set eyes are not to be trusted.

By the time we reach adolescence, we have been thoroughly schooled in these standards. The Dallas Cowboys' cheerleaders, small- and big-screen "jiggle shows," Barbie and Ken dolls, magazines like *Seventeen* for adolescents and *Vogue* for their moms, and beauty contests that begin in infancy are only the beginnings of the vast body-image brainwashing we receive.

Growing up on such an insistent diet of beautiful face and body imagery, it's no wonder Dick and Jane feel inadequate by the time they reach the teen years. They have mirrors. They understand they probably can't measure up. Sadly, Dick and Jane have been well indoctrinated to believe that beautiful faces and bodies are what count in life, along with athletic ability and money for "in" apparel.

Madison Avenue continues to shape our values as adults. In a slide-lecture entitled "The Naked Truth: Advertising's Image of Women" (the results grew out of ten years of research on sex role stereotyping in advertising), Dr. Jean Kilbourne says, "Ads are selling something besides products. They're selling values, images, and concepts of love, sexuality, romance, and success. More importantly, they are telling us who we are and what we should be."

Kilbourne accuses beauty ads of contributing to our youth-oriented culture (young is beautiful and beautiful is young) and of setting a standard of beauty that is impossible to attain—just as movies and novels do, but with more impact: "Ads tell us that we are basically ugly in our natural state, and we must learn to disguise ourselves with cosmetics. They teach us to spend time and money on beauty, and to feel guilty if we don't."

Without this basic equipment, we're programmed to believe, only a great personality can win you friends. The problem is, of course, that the child or adult who thinks he is ugly has a hard time feeling outgoing and friendly and fun.

Since the point of all advertising is to make us feel dissatisfied with who we are and what we have, and we are under such a constant barrage of it, perhaps it's not surprising that even in adulthood we continue to entertain distorted ideas of what really matters. We *are* susceptible to the standards so insistently projected on the screens of our minds.

WHAT OUR FAMILY SAYS

Obesity, boniness, a large nose, protruding ears, acne, thick or thin lips, baldness, tallness, shortness, squatness—these and every other conceivable "imperfection" are targets for our peers while we are growing up. Few of us escape the name-calling and labeling that magnify any flaw and imprint it on our minds forever. Everyone feels ugly sometimes, and everyone remembers some teasing aimed at his face and body.

Nan's brother and parents, for instance, tease her about her big nose. Her boyfriend assures her that she's pretty, but, she says, "All I can see in the mirror is my nose." How many times is that kind of teasing duplicated in otherwise loving homes?

Not only so-called innocent teasing, but even the most casual comment can cause us to focus on our supposed imperfections. Your daughter comments one day that she has Mom's round nose. If you previously had been unaware of that particular flaw, now you see it clearly in every mirror, in every photo.

Such casual comments are sometimes unbelievably insensitive, especially when aimed at vulnerable children:

My sister and I are close in age and height, but she's as skinny as I am happy. My uncle jokes a lot about my being too selfish to give her some of my extra weight. He says I must keep all the food to myself. I guess he thinks he's being funny.

Well-meaning adults with false values can cause deep harm:

My twin sister died when we were small, and I overheard a relative say, "Isn't it a shame the pretty one died?" I grew up feeling guilty, knowing I must be a disappointment to my parents because I could never measure up to my sister's looks.

Even right values—modesty, for example—can be taught in a destructive way:

My parents didn't allow me to use a mirror when I was growing up, and they told me I was nothing to look at anyway. They said, "You really have nothing to be proud of, you know." My brothers picked up on that and were allowed to taunt me. I've always felt very ugly. Consequently, I have assumed that my husband says I'm pretty only because that's what husbands are supposed to say. It's hard to believe that others might consider me attractive.

There's a case of devout, but deeply mistaken, parents trying to insulate their child against the sin of pride. Instead, they inflicted on her the pain of imagined ugliness.

A UNIVERSAL PLAGUE

As hard as it is to believe, the same malady afflicts everyone. Even the beautiful sometimes find it difficult to like themselves and to believe that others accept them, too. All the world pays attention to a beautiful child, but the response changes when the child grows into an adult. People tend to feel intimidated by unusually attractive people, so they hesitate to include them in their circle of friends.

Unfortunately, the attention an attractive person receives is usually based on his good looks rather than his kind and caring behavior. This can reinforce a sense of self-preoccupation and block his awareness of the esteem needs of others.

He may not learn how to develop the close friendships we all need to assure us we're OK.

It is perhaps easier to see how the unappealing or deformed person can develop the kind of self-focus that shuts others out. Fearing rejection, he finds it difficult to reach out beyond his own safe world. Without practice, he becomes socially inadequate. He would find it hard to believe that his most attractive acquaintance might also be lonely and fearful.

WHEN OTHERS THINK YOU'RE UGLY

At least beautiful people are treated better by society. In an article entitled "All the Homely People," Gregg Lewis documents how people judge unattractive strangers to be unhappy, cold, insensitive, and dull. And that isn't all.

- Personnel managers are slower to hire unattractive people, and they pay them less.
- Jurors consider them to be less believable on the witness stand.
- Judges give them longer prison sentences.
- Hospitals and mental institutions give them less attention and more serious diagnoses.[1]

Other research indicates that both academic grades and behavioral correction in the classroom are influenced by the attractiveness of a student! And it's not only teachers; other adults also suspect the unattractive child of being more dishonest and more likely to cause trouble than the attractive child.[2]

Unfortunately, the conclusion of these adults is often correct, since an unattractive child must learn to cope in some way with the rejection he faces. As a result, physical defects often lead to emotional problems.

There is an old line that goes, "Beauty is only skin deep, but ugliness goes clear to the bone." It might be more accurate to say, "Ugliness goes clear to the soul." The effects of ugliness plow deep into a person's self-image and personality. And the reactions of other people can cripple an unattractive person in every area of his or her life.[3]

No one could read this stark commentary by Moses Chase without feeling pain:

You don't find it on the top-forty charts, but the sound of ugliness is heard any place people gather. The first line goes, "He/she is nice, but . . ." And in the silence after "but," if you listen, you can hear all the sounds of pain that every ugly-feeling person hears. The sound of ugliness is seldom audible, seldom so gross as "I can't stand to look at him," or "What a dog!"—although you can hear remarks like that.

The sound of ugliness is mostly silent. You can hear it when people's conversation stops as a crippled person crosses their path. You can hear it when a girl sits next to a guy with pimples and automatically turns to the person on the other side, not wanting, really, to talk to a guy who looks like that and is so awkward and uncomfortable about himself. You can hear it in the hesitation in the moment before a guy slides into the back-seat of a car, jammed in next to the girl who's overweight. The fat people can hear it. The people with harelips can hear it. The people with plain faces or skeletons the wrong size or bodies that lack the right shape can hear it. And if the sound of ugliness could be heard all the time, by everyone, it would make such a chorus of groanings, of self-hating sighs, of sadness, that I think we could hear very little of anything else.[4]

HOW WE JUDGE OTHERS

Each of us feels the sting of rejection when others judge us by the world's ungodly standards of attractiveness. But aren't we guilty of imposing those same standards on others? Don't we too contribute to the pain of the unattractive? About 10 percent of the population apparently falls into the unattractive or unappealing category, and *Campus Life* asks some disturbing questions:

Following the 10 percent guideline, if there are thirty people in your English class, three of them could be classified as unattractive. Do you make any effort to be friendly with these three people? Or do you even think about them? . . . Who are the people in your school you'd most like to associate with? . . . We like to think we're concerned about more than physical attractiveness, but looks are usually the major factor. . . . The prejudices are imbedded deeply into our culture. But if we recognize the prejudice for what it is, we may reduce some of the hurt and the injustice. . . .[5]

Our rejection of unlovely people isn't usually a conscious cruelty. Our tendency is to overlook them—and that is perceived as rejection. Unconscious it may be, but cruelty it remains. We're so anxious not to stare at the deformed and defective that we ignore them instead. That's rejection.

There are unattractive people in the world who hurt, who withdraw from relationships, who may never reach the potential God created them for. . . . If I believe God created human beings in his own image, I have to recognize that some of that image is present in every person I know—even the most unattractive people. My responsibility as a Christian is to help bring out and build up that image in myself and others. . . .[6]

This may be our responsibility, but we certainly fail at it! It's so easy to accept the standards Satan has built into our world's system and to forget or ignore God's values. And that failure is exactly what makes us susceptible to unhealthy self-esteem.

ARE YOU BEAUTIFUL?
When God sent Samuel to find his choice of Israel's next king, seven of Jesse's eight sons were paraded before

Samuel. Samuel's eyes focused on Eliab, who must have been tall and handsome and muscular—everything the world admires—because Samuel's reaction was, "Surely this is the man the Lord has chosen!" (1 Sam. 16:6, TLB).

How many women have had the same reaction to such a man? How many men have responded this way to a beautiful woman and lived to regret it?

God's response to Samuel is very plain: "Don't judge by a man's face or height, for this is not the one. I don't make decisions the way you do! Men judge by outward appearance, but I look at a man's thoughts and intentions" (1 Sam. 16:7, TLB).

The message is clear, but we haven't learned it very well. God created some beautiful faces and bodies, but Scripture doesn't indicate that these characteristics make a person more important or valuable than anyone else.

Let's work to change our standards. Far more important than physical beauty are the qualities God cherishes! Physical beauty is a mockery if it houses an unlovely spirit, but good character qualities can make anyone seem beautiful. Cultivate that inner attractiveness yourself and look for it in every person you meet! God's Word is specific:

Don't be concerned about the outward beauty that depends on jewelry, or beautiful clothes, or hair arrangement. Be beautiful inside, in your hearts, with the lasting charm of a gentle and quiet spirit which is so precious to God. (1 Pet. 3:3-4, TLB)

There are some things we can do to improve our appearance, of course, since we all do have to live in this world. We can work on posture, try different hairstyles, and learn what colors and clothing styles bring out our good features.

But each of us has a God-given face and body, and we can't change our bone structure, the width of our mouths, or the size of our feet.

Make the best of what you have, but don't let your appearance drag you down or consume your life. You are worth a lot more than your face and figure! Whose judgment will you value—the world's or God's?

QUESTIONS FOR PERSONAL APPLICATION

1. How does your body image today affect your self-worth?
2. What comments have affected your view of your appearance?
3. Think of someone you know whom you see as physically unattractive. How would your feelings toward that person change if he were to become very attractive? How might you act differently?
4. How might you help unattractive people reach the potential for which God created them? Be specific.
5. How have the standards of advertising affected your values? Are there changes you need to make?
6. Knowing that we have to live in this world, is there something you could do to improve your appearance? How will this change affect your self-esteem?
7. Is there some way you can help your children feel more accepted by improving their appearance without creating undue focus on their looks?
8. What qualities of inward beauty does God's Word encourage Christians to seek after? (See 1 Pet. 3:1-9; Matt. 5:3-9; Rom. 12:9-21; Eph. 4:1-3, 22-32; Phil. 2:3-4.)
9. Do you spend more time improving your physical appearance or your inner beauty? How could you adapt your daily schedule to give priority to developing those qualities God calls beautiful?

QUESTIONS FOR GROUP DISCUSSION

1. In what subtle ways do we encourage a preoccupation with body image?
2. Do you think God is interested in our maintaining an attractive physical appearance? What leads you to this conclusion? Discuss how to achieve a balance between enhancing our appearance and placing an undue emphasis on beauty.
3. How did you feel about your appearance when you were in junior high school? What made you feel that way?
4. Do you recall any teasing or hurtful comments about your appearance? How did they affect your self-esteem, and for how long did they have that effect?
5. Recall the physically beautiful people you have known. What is your perception of their self-esteem? Would you be as prone to reach out in friendship to someone who is beautiful as you would to a more ordinary-looking person? Why?

6. Consider the statements from "All the Homely People" on pages 47 and 49. Discuss why people would hold such prejudices.
7. If it is our responsibility as Christians to help bring out and build up God's image in ourselves and others, how can we do that?
8. Discuss some of the values, images, and concepts ads sell us. What do they tell us about who we are and what we should be?
9. Discuss question 8 from Questions for Personal Application.

5 I'm Susceptible: How Smart Am I?
Your Intelligence and Self-Esteem

*If you clerk in a store or run a switchboard or work in a
service station, people assume it's because you're not bright
enough to go to college.*

*I want to operate a dog kennel, but everyone is telling me
I'm too intelligent for that; I have to use my education. Trans-
lated: I'll be respected more if my vocation demonstrates my
intelligence. But running a dog kennel is what I want to do.
Why do I need to feel I'm not fulfilling my potential when I'm
doing something I enjoy?*

INTELLIGENCE EQUALS WORTH?

It seems that the more advanced our technology becomes,
the more we must prove our abilities in order to prove our
value as people. Intelligence ranks highest on the list, of
course, especially if we accept the prevailing humanistic
philosophy:

- Each person makes himself what he is.
- Each person is responsible only to himself.
- Each person can solve his problems independently of God.

According to the "Humanist Manifesto II," the next century will provide humanity with unparalleled opportunity for achieving abundant and meaningful lives.

If an "abundant and meaningful life" is attainable through human capabilities alone, then the spotlight is necessarily on those who have the highest level of knowledge and skills. And as fields of learning grow more specialized, education will become an even more critical factor in self-evaluation. As that happens, who will be more valuable to society—the research scientist or the laborer? The Phi Beta Kappa member or the mentally handicapped student?

This philosophy isn't new, it's just increasing in intensity. As it continues to escalate, intelligence will become an even more critical factor in self-evaluation in many circles. Increasingly, how others treat us will be determined by our brain power, making us more and more susceptible to feelings of inferiority or superiority.

If you're like most people, you won't be as pressured by the intelligence-equals-worth credo *if your esteem needs are being met elsewhere.* But if you're either a brain or a slow learner, your focus of attention will probably remain fixed on the needs created by your feelings of being different from others.

WHEN INTELLIGENCE COUNTS TOO MUCH

Brilliance produces a unique set of difficulties. It's lonely at the top. When asked how being gifted had most affected his life, Roger had a simple answer: "Social isolation."

It began in grade school when his exploring mind led him toward pursuits that didn't match those of the other boys his age. When schoolwork was graded on a curve, classmates further isolated him, blaming him for dragging down their grades. By the time he reached junior high, peer approval had become important enough that he deliberately did inferior work in order to gain acceptance. But the pattern was set. He was—well—different. And different is an ugly label in junior and senior high school.

S. Rickly Christian describes the experience of another gifted student:

Mark was the kind of guy you loved to hate. He wore wing tips, played chess during lunch, submitted his research papers on sixteenth-century Huguenots for publication in history journals and debated with the science teacher about obscure facts in the textbook. Everybody figured he'd be the school valedictorian, attend an Ivy League university on a full academic scholarship, and do graduate work abroad.

But that never happened. In his junior year, Mark got tired of everybody thinking he was different from them. He didn't want to be thought of as some freak genius. He wanted to be just a regular guy. And in his mind "regular" meant drinking, smoking, and partying. He started playing dumb in class and didn't even seem fazed when his grades dropped to Cs. He exchanged his calculator pouch for a tobacco pouch and studied Zen instead of Huguenots and inert gases.

Even though I'd resented Mark for distorting the class curves, I felt sad watching him succumb to peer pressure and become just another face in the crowd. I kept hoping he'd come to his senses, but that never happened. He never even took the SAT college entrance exam. Instead of pursuing a brilliant future, he took a job at a beach snack shop. And whenever I think of peer pressure and its effects, I think of Mark sitting in his stand selling 45-cent snow cones.[1]

If loneliness is often a way of life for the intellectually gifted, it can be more so for the intellectually deprived. John is a slow learner, and he *knows* he doesn't measure up. He has met failure all his life; he has been ridiculed, snubbed, and ignored. Now as an adult, the only work he can find isn't usually something he can be proud of. There is no hope of getting ahead or, for that matter, even catching up.

John isn't alone. Dr. James Dobson says in *Hide or Seek:*

The categories of learning problems . . . (slow learner, semi-literate, underachiever, culturally deprived, and late bloomer) represent the five large groups of students who consistently fail in the classroom. It is appalling to recognize that the children in these categories actually outnumber those students who feel successful in school! *This means that personal dissatisfaction and disappointment are very common products of our educational system. It accounts for the large percentage of adults in our society who secretly "know" they are stupid—the one lesson learned best from their school days.*[2]

Tragically, many of these adults have fulfilled a prophecy of failure.

LEARNING STARTS AT HOME

How does a healthy—or unhealthy—attitude toward intelligence develop? A sense of achievement must begin at home, but parents can't pass on to their children what they themselves don't have. If they are hopelessly trapped in their own feelings of low self-esteem, they may find it difficult to be encouraging, and take little interest in activities that would help the children become better students. This will subtly communicate to their children that there is little hope of achievement.

At the other extreme, low-achieving parents may push children toward unrealistic goals with the hope of achieving vicariously through them. And when the children don't measure up, everyone loses.

Parents who are high achievers may also set impossible standards for their children. Their inevitable disappointment erodes their children's self-confidence further.

Parents, as well as teachers, need to have a healthy attitude toward intelligence. What is the balance between accepting a child's current abilities and encouraging him to stretch toward his potential?

We must first recognize this key fact: Intelligence is not a basis for self-esteem, but a gift to be encouraged.

With this in mind, perhaps we need to examine the basis of our encouragement. Are we possibly buying into society's values? Could we really be seeking greater status or greater recognition—for them or for us as parents? Or do we encourage our children to make the most of their gifts for their own personal satisfaction and the knowledge that they've done their best? The last motive is the only one that provides a basis for healthy self-esteem.

As you encourage your children, they may indicate in every possible way that they don't care what you think. Don't you believe it! Your opinion of them matters deeply. Emotional ties to parents are strong and deep, even in children who have been neglected or abused or even deserted. A parent's assessment (communicated mainly through attitudes) can effectively enhance or inhibit a child's potential. If your own parents don't believe in you, who will?

HOW TEACHERS HELP—OR HURT

Children desperately want the approval of authority figures—parents first and then teachers. A child needs to know that his teachers respect and value him. He needs to feel he belongs, whether he is an extrovert or an introvert, a good student or a struggler. He needs to feel competent at his own level.

After only one month of school, Tammy's kindergarten teacher, impatient because the child could not yet print her name, began sending notes home accusing the parents of not putting forth their best efforts to help. Tammy was being ordered to write her name on the blackboard in front of the class, a task she could not accomplish. Tammy's enjoyment of school was spoiled by her teacher's methods; the critical notes undercut not only her self-esteem, but also her parents'. Incentives are necessary, but pressure to perform takes the joy out of learning.

Teachers (and parents) can harm the self-esteem of a child through:

- being sarcastic,
- giving put-downs,
- using embarrassing motivational methods,
- showing insensitivity to real needs,
- ignoring a child's presence,
- having pets,
- correcting behavior with verbal attacks.

One study has revealed that 75 percent of a teacher's comments to students are negative, even though it takes four positive statements to offset the effects of one negative comment to a child.

Soon after our daughter entered fifth grade, her enthusiastic, happy attitude toward school did a complete reversal. She no longer cared to spend extra time on special assignments; she didn't even care if she did the required work.

We discovered that embarrassing put-downs were just one of her teacher's negative motivational methods, and although Brenda wasn't usually his target, she was suffering on behalf of other students who were. Promised parties and excursions were repeatedly withheld from the entire class because of only one child's misdemeanor; they missed every fun event the other classes enjoyed. We prayed her through the year and tried to support her in special ways, not dreaming that God would turn this negative experience into a positive!

When Brenda became a teenager, we began to notice that she had an unusual ability to cope with the pains and disappointments teenagers face. Her experiences in fifth grade seemed to have enabled her to avoid naive expectations that bring needless heartbreak, and she was able to see that God had used her difficult year for her good.

The encouragement of caring parents can minimize the damage done by an occasional insensitive teacher. But some children don't have support either at home or at school. Negative learning experiences can mutilate their self-esteem so much that they never have a chance to succeed.

After spending his first year of high school in three different special education programs, Terrance Swilley was kicked out of the public school system (in Chicago) as unteachable. He had a straight-F average.

The school board placed him . . . at the Academy of St. James College Preparatory School, a private inner-city school for grades 1 through 12 that stresses strict discipline, self-respect, and basic learning skills.

Swilley graduated from the academy with a straight-A average, as a member of the National Honor Society, and now attends the Illinois Institute of Technology, where he is studying aeronautical engineering.[3]

What was the difference in this school that brought about such a dramatic change? St. James Academy was organized in 1970 by the Rev. Barnell G. Smith because he recognized, after years of teaching in inner-city schools, that "an important need of inner-city kids was not being met . . . [the need for] *self-respect and self-esteem.*"[4]

Teachers have a remarkable opportunity to influence students' attitudes toward themselves and others. Teachers can add fuel to the fires of criticism and ridicule, or sow the seeds of compassion and understanding. They can build up or tear down the self-esteem of their students, often with long-lasting effects.

THE FREEDOM TO FAIL

Some form of humiliation seems inescapable during the school years. Whether or not scholastic standing was important to you, what *was* important was that it not bring embarrassment. If other children made fun of you because of the reading group you were in, if you were humiliated in front of the class because you answered wrong and caused your team to lose, or if you were criticized by the teacher in front of your peers, your self-esteem was zapped. How many embarrassing moments we remember from childhood!

Children need to be taught that life is a learning process and that they are bound to make mistakes sometimes. If everyone knew all the right answers and the right behaviors, there would be no room for growth. If only we would recognize this truth! Randy Stonehill, a Christian rock star, told an interviewer:

I was afraid of venturing into other areas because I was afraid of failure. I wish I'd had a different perspective. I wish somebody had told me that it's OK to be who you are and fail. That just identifies you with the human race. But you see a lot of people—maybe the majority—who aren't sure it is OK to fail, because their image is all they have to cling to.[5]

We must help children understand that:

- We all goof.
- We're still OK even when we fail.
- It helps to laugh at ourselves.

And maybe God lovingly laughs with us.

Grown-ups need to learn these lessons, too!

THE BEST KNOWLEDGE
Society's value of intelligence is in a profit- and success-oriented world. It is certainly valid if people think they are going to solve the world's problems independently of God! But are we?

So what about these wise men, these scholars, these brilliant debaters of this world's great affairs? God has made them all look foolish, and shown their wisdom to be useless nonsense. (1 Cor. 1:20, TLB)

The world may consider the research scientists and the Phi Beta Kappas more valuable than others, but apparently God doesn't. His evaluation doesn't seem to depend on intelligence any more than on looks. Surely he expects us to use to the utmost the abilities he has given us, but his love doesn't depend on what they are or how fully we use them!

Your knowledge of the world is not important to God. It's your knowledge of him and your relationship with him that matter most. To know him you don't have to excel in the world's wisdom; you only need to acknowledge his Son as Savior and Lord.

For God in his wisdom saw to it that the world would never find God through human brilliance, and then he stepped in and saved all those who believed his message, which the world calls foolish and silly. (1 Cor. 1:21, TLB)

Imagine the head of a large corporation choosing men like the twelve apostles to be his assistants! The disciples were mostly uneducated men, yet Jesus poured his life into them. He trained them and entrusted to them the most important message in the history of the world. If those twelve men had failed to comprehend the message and pass it on, Christianity would have died in the cradle. They were far from intellectual giants, yet they fulfilled Jesus' expectations—they did what he asked *through his empowerment.*

It's a tough assignment we have, to live in this world and yet not allow its emphasis on intelligence and academic achievement to undermine or puff up our self-worth. But we can do it if we keep our attention focused on God's values and his standards. We can do it if we consciously and deliberately work to change our personal criteria for the answer to that question, "How smart am I?"

QUESTIONS FOR PERSONAL APPLICATION

1. How did your parents react to your achievement—or lack of it—in school? What effect did their reaction have on you?
2. How did you feel about yourself in school? What did your teachers do to give you that feeling?
3. What incidents do you recall that made you feel smart or dumb?
4. Embarrassing incidents that keep popping into your mind can affect your self-worth. How can you correct your self-talk regarding those occasions?
5. In what areas does peer pressure influence your attitudes and decisions? How has it affected you this past week?
6. In what ways might your self-esteem be affecting your children's intellectual development?
7. What can be changed in your home environment to give your children confidence in themselves?
8. Are you as a parent or teacher using any of the wrong methods listed on page 58? How will you change?
9. If you're a teacher, ask a close friend or an understanding parent to record your critical and favorable comments in class for a day or a half day. How did your pupils fare? How would they have fared if you hadn't been conscious of being recorded?

QUESTIONS FOR GROUP DISCUSSION

1. Discuss situations at work, at school, at home, and in your community that are affected by a high value being placed on intelligence.
2. Discuss why the intelligence-equals-worth credo is not important to an individual whose esteem needs are being met elsewhere.
3. How can we help a gifted student accept his "differentness"?
4. How can we teach children to accept slow learners and be kind to those who are different from them in some way?
5. Discuss how parents with low self-esteems might hinder the development of their children's potential. How might high-achieving parents or parents who cope by acting superior do the same?
6. What good motivational methods did your teachers use? What poor ones?
7. List ways we can help our families accept their mistakes as part of a learning process.
8. Discuss what parents can do to build self-confidence in family

members and help cushion the blows to self-esteem received at
school, work, and play.

9. Read Job 28:28; Psalm 119:98-100; Matthew 7:24; 2 Timothy 3:15;
   James 1:5; 3:17. What do these verses teach us about wisdom?

6   I'm Susceptible: What's My Status?
Your Socioeconomic Success and Self-Esteem

A high school girl reports, with some bitterness:

In my school your dad's money and profession determine your importance. The cheerleaders and beauty queens are all rich kids.

Social standing and financial position seem to go hand in hand with degree of importance in American society. Success is being anyone at the top; cheerleaders, beauty queens, leaders in business, and the Beautiful People of the gossip columns all qualify. Since those at the top usually have money, wealth often appears to be the key to a successful life. So many people keep reaching for the star of economic success, thinking it will bring "happily-ever-aftering." Struggling, straining, yearning. For success. For money.

THE VIEW FROM THE TOP
But financial success doesn't necessarily make us happy with ourselves. It doesn't always provide the full and meaningful life we seek. Ask those at the top.

In 1923 a group of the world's most successful financiers

met at the Edgewater Beach Hotel in Chicago. Collectively, these tycoons controlled more wealth than the United States Treasury. Newspapers and magazines printed their success stories, urging young people to follow their examples. Were their lives meaningful?

1. Charles Schwab, *president of the largest independent steel company: lived on borrowed money for the last five years of his life and died penniless.*
2. Arthur Cutten, *the greatest wheat speculator: died abroad insolvent.*
3. Richard Whitney, *president of the New York Stock Exchange: imprisoned in Sing Sing.*
4. Albert Fall, *a member of the president's cabinet: imprisoned, then pardoned so he could die at home.*
5. Jesse Livermore, *the greatest bear in Wall Street: suicide.*
6. Leon Fraser, *president of the Bank of International Settlement: suicide.*
7. Ivar Krueger, *head of the world's greatest monopoly: suicide.*[1]

Three suicides out of that small circle of "successful" men, known and respected worldwide. They knew how to make money, but they apparently didn't find their lives either meaningful or valuable.

Personalities in the entertainment world also give clear evidence that money, success, and reknown cannot be equated with happiness or a sense of worthwhileness. The high rates of suicide, drug abuse, and divorce among recognized performers do not speak of satisfaction based on socioeconomic status.

HOW OTHERS SIZE US UP
Lack of money and status are often accompanied by a corresponding lack of self-esteem. We compare many aspects of our lives with our friends:

- Our occupation
- Our place of residence
- Our style of dress
- Our choice of car
- Our use of leisure time
- Our possessions
- Our social life

It's what others *appear* to have that affects our attitude toward them and about ourselves when we're with them. Although people all have different priorities for the use of their money, we judge others' economic status according to how they spend what they have. We tend to feel defensive and intimidated or less worthy when we're with those who appear to be in a higher income bracket or level of education than we are. In contrast, we may feel comfortably superior when we're with those who may have less money or less education than we do. Even in church circles we hesitate to be friendly with the wealthy or the poor. And we make that judgment without knowing all the facts.

So we size up others as we meet them, and we sense they're doing the same to us.

In an old cartoon, a woman confides to her husband's pal: "Your friendship means so much to Harold. You're the only one he knows who makes less than he does!"

Our attitude toward someone can change, subtly or drastically, when we learn his or her occupation. For that reason, we hesitate to share certain aspects of our lives if we think others might find them unworthy and judge us accordingly.

THE HOUSEWIFE BLUES
"Do you work?"
   "No, I'm *only* a housewife."
Is a housewife, then, less intelligent than business and professional women? Are housewives less valuable than working women?

These questions are being asked by more and more homemakers today. Many are responding by returning to the job market. Their need to feel successful is often greater than their need for money! The drive for what they may call personal fulfillment is often a need for personal status—a sense of contributing something to society and so proving their worth.

Her role clashes head-on with the real values of an achievement-oriented culture. Furthermore, Mother has no credentials. She is an unpaid amateur, and this gives her low status in a society obsessed with professional, certified expertise. . . . There are no effective yardsticks by which to measure the quality of a mother's work.[2]

Linda speaks for many homemakers when she says: "Mother's job has no status in a society which rewards the single-minded pursuit of money and success," says educator Grace Hechinger in *Newsweek*.

I feel like a nobody. My appearance doesn't even matter to me anymore. Why should it? My kids don't care, and my husband is too wrapped up in his work to notice. I need to know if I'm worth anything beyond wiping noses, sorting socks, and refereeing arguments. I have to at least try proving myself at a job.

Though Linda and many other women think they'll gain status by joining the work force, they may find that, in reality, it only adds to the problem. At a 1981 midwestern women's conference, Dr. Jean Kilbourne charged that the women's movement has brought about a new stereotype, the I-can-do-it-all superwoman, which is subtly reinforced by advertising.

"The message is clear," said Dr. Kilbourne. "You've got to be beautiful, a good wife and mother, and hold a job outside the home. And if you can't cope with all that, you haven't got your act together."

Even if Linda does manage to cope with her new superwoman role, others may feel uncomfortable with her new status and subtly withdraw from her. What her self-esteem gains in one way may be lost in other ways.

STATUS SYMBOLS

Status symbols affect us all. We may become intimidated when we're invited to a home that is larger and more expensively furnished than ours; we may hesitate to reciprocate that hospitality.

We feel uncomfortable and inadequate around people who are always in the latest fashion. So we may spend more for clothes than we can actually afford, hoping to achieve the right look. Every teenage girl knows which shop is the "in" place for clothes, and those who can't afford to buy there feel inferior to those who do. Even kindergarteners cry for designer labels so they will have standing among their peers.

Men will more likely seek to impress others with the car they buy. The make and the model considered prestigious differs with both generation and geography. Status to a young Coloradan is a Jeep; to a Texan, a pickup truck; to many midwesterners, a van; and to the country club set anywhere, a foreign sports car.

Even where and how you exercise can be a matter of status. You may seek to join the most expensive health club in order to be seen with all the "right" people.

Some people take the opposite tack—they want everyone to know that they refuse to play this people-pleasing game. John, for instance, painted the inside of his house before he painted the outside because he wanted to prove that he didn't want to impress people! A missionary serving in the U.S., when presented with a personal shower of lovely clothes, promptly returned them, believing she had to dress from the missionary barrel in order to be a true servant of God. These are commendable values, yet we have to watch that even they don't become a source of pride.

FINDING A BALANCE

Whether or not God has blessed us financially, we don't have to dress and act as though he hasn't in order to prove that our values are right. Nor should we need to have the latest in fashion and gadgets to feel valuable. A balance is in order. The most important consideration is a nonjudgmental attitude toward others, no matter where we or they are on the economic scale.

Our friends, Marilyn and Cal, are good examples. When a progressively debilitating illness struck Cal several years ago, they were forced to give up their beautiful home in the "right" neighborhood and go on disability pay. When asked how this affected their self-esteem, Marilyn replied:

At first our eyes were on ourselves as we struggled to get on top of the situation. Cal, especially, was suffering loss of self-esteem because he was becoming unable to do even little things for himself, like getting his keys out of his pocket. He could no longer be part of the work force, and this made him feel he was losing his manhood.

It was a humbling experience for me to seek financial aid. I refused to deliberately look needy and was met with contempt when I went to the welfare office dressed in hose and heels.

The turning point for us came when God showed us in James 1:2 that sooner or later everyone will be faced with a trial that seems monumental, and when it comes we must make choices. We realized that we had been dwelling on what we couldn't do, what we couldn't have, what we had to give up. So we did an about-face, and chose, instead, to dwell on what we could do, on what we did have. We chose not to wallow in self-pity. When your eyes get on yourself, you're in trouble. We laugh a lot because we've chosen to keep our sense of humor and not let our circumstances get us down.

Marilyn and Cal credit this illness with a dramatic change in their values. They now recognize that their worth isn't determined by where they live, the car they drive, or what they wear, but they don't call attention to themselves in order to prove this point. Though they have limited funds, they know how to fit into the world without buying into its value system. They don't have designer clothes, but they use well what they are given. Their daughters blend in with the others in their high school and are among the most popular, as are their parents, because they have learned not to be concerned with things, but with people.

Marilyn and Cal are such examples of victory and joy that others in much better circumstances continually seek their counsel. Their phone rings constantly, and there is a steady stream of people dropping by their home, some with heavy burdens, some just desiring a few moments in that warm, joyful, accepting atmosphere. And it's all because of their attitude—humble, centered on God and on others.

It's easier to be accepted in this world when we adapt, within Christian standards, to the culture in which we live. Missionaries, for example, work hard at fitting into the culture around them. But in this process, we don't have to *accept* the values of that culture, using its socioeconomic scale to judge value—our own or others.

When Christ chose the Twelve, their economic status was no more a factor than their intelligence or education. No business tycoons or millionaires in that little group, as far as we know. No corporate giants—just a few men with hearts to follow Jesus, probably facing ridicule as they abandoned their livelihoods. For the sake of Christ they sacrificed whatever status they may have attained in the community.

FINAL SUCCESS

This life is relatively short. Ultimately, our success in life will be totally removed from our status here. God speaks to the issue clearly and repeatedly. In Proverbs we read that the wisdom of God is more profitable than riches. In Jesus' eyes, the widow's tiny gift, representing all she had, was worth far more than the large gifts of the rich. Paul said it all in Philippians 3:7, "But whatever things were gain to me, those things I have counted as loss for the sake of Christ" (NASB).

When we come to the end of our lives, we will take with us nothing that the world has labeled an evidence of success. We will stand before God stripped of makeup, expensive clothes, bank account, business title, and briefcase. What measure of success will we possess? Only the one exemplified by Jesus. At the end of his life here, he declared, "I glorified Thee on the earth, having accomplished the work which Thou hast given Me to do" (John 17:4, NASB).

We are told in Scripture to glorify God in whatever we do. We glorify God when our attitudes and actions show that we are confident enough in him to obey him and live for him. Truly successful people are those who glorify God by allowing him to use their lives according to the potential he has supplied.

We'll become less and less susceptible to unhealthy self-esteem when the only status we seek is found in God's "Well done, thou good and faithful servant" (Matt. 25:21, KJV). As we rid ourselves of the empty, meaningless standards for success that prevail in the business and social world—and even in the church — we can encourage instead godly standards. Watch them spill over into the schoolroom and the playground and the office!

QUESTIONS FOR PERSONAL APPLICATION

1. How is your self-esteem influenced by your occupation? Your husband's occupation? Do you place greater value on some occupations than you do on others?
2. Is your evaluation of a person influenced by his place of residence? Style of dress? Use of leisure time? Possessions?
3. Does a person's economic level affect whether or not you reach out to him?
4. What is your idea of success? Are you successful?
5. In what specific areas do you need to free yourself from conformity to the world's standards of success?
6. How can you incorporate godly values into your day-to-day living?
7. Answer question 4 from Questions for Group Discussion.

QUESTIONS FOR GROUP DISCUSSION

1. What effect does a person's appearance of wealth have on your interaction with him? How can you extend friendship to people at both ends of the economic scale?
2. In what ways should we adapt to our culture? In what ways should we be different? How can we keep from judging ourselves and others by the standards of our culture?
3. What do you think constitutes success?
4. What are God's standards for success? See Josh. 1:8; Ps. 1; 103:14-18; Prov. 3:13-26; 4:5-9; 22:1; Matt. 6:26-33; Rom. 12:2; Phil. 3:7-14; 4:11-13. Can you think of other references? Is it possible for everyone to achieve these standards?

7 I'm Susceptible: How Well Am I Liked?
Your Personality and Self-Esteem

Miss Evans, our Brownie leader, seemed to really like us. She was a warm, gracious redhead, and my sisters and I figured she was probably the most gorgeous lady in the world. Years later we learned that our beautiful Miss Evans had been a quite homely woman with a henna rinse. We saw her as beautiful because we liked her. Because she liked us.

What draws you to other people? Their appearance? Their good taste or good grooming? Their level of intelligence? Their position on the social scale or their income? All of these things may help determine your selection of friends. But it is another's personality that really solidifies your reaction to him. We might even say that it's mainly your personality that determines your popularity.

The desire to be popular is universal. "Do they like me?" we worry. We all long to be liked and appreciated for what we are. We all need to feel included. And our personality is the most important aspect in determining whether we will find the acceptance that is necessary to self-esteem.

Your self-esteem affects every aspect of your personality,

and your personality helps determine your self-esteem because of the response it produces.

Let's explore personality. What makes up the person inside the body we wear? How do our personality traits influence self-esteem?

TEMPERAMENT

Your temperament is one aspect of your personality. Ever since Hippocrates, an ancient Greek scholar, first developed the temperament theory, people have been perceived as falling into one of four categories. You are basically sanguine, choleric, melancholic, phlegmatic, or some combination of the four.

The most popular person is usually the one who is predominantly sanguine. It's fun to be with someone who is humorous, carefree, outgoing, and enthusiastic. The only one who might feel uncomfortable around a sanguine is a quiet or insecure person, especially if the sanguine is overly helpful, confident, or boisterous. However, the sanguine is usually too optimistic to notice one less admirer.

The self-esteem of the uninvolved, indifferent phlegmatic is also not often trampled on. He is easygoing, calm, and comfortable—a person easy to accept and love. He may be ignored because of his quiet and unassuming manner, but he would be less likely to consider this a blow to his self-esteem than would the melancholy.

The melancholy is inclined to be moody and withdrawn, and is apt to be left alone for fear of wounding his sensitive spirit. Because melancholies are introspective and overly analytical, they are likely to blow out of proportion anything remotely resembling a slight or an affront. It's worth trying to understand melancholies, though, for they are thoughtful and creative.

The choleric may not always recognize it, but one of his greatest needs is to be accepted. Although he is respected for his leadership and organizational skills, his unsympathetic, opinionated, aggressive approach may not win him many friends.

People with melancholic and choleric temperaments are probably those with the least healthy self-esteems. Unhealthy self-esteem is manifested in the melancholy with feelings of inferiority and in the choleric with feelings of superiority.

The more our temperament is under the control of the Holy Spirit, the more our negative characteristics will be softened, and our humble centering on others will draw them to us.

Understanding the temperaments of our family members and close associates can make the difference in whether we accept or reject their behavior; it can eliminate much of the criticism we heap upon them.

For years I was frustrated by my husband's indifference to just about everything but me. I kept trying to get a response, to motivate him to become involved. Then I learned about the temperaments and quickly recognized his phlegmatic characteristics. The traits I so love—his calmness, his dependability, and his easygoing, unassuming nature—are also part of the temperament I had been complaining about. I'm so glad I learned this; what a difference it has made in our relationship! Now I love him for all of it and wonder how he has put up with my melancholic-choleric temperament all these years!

ABILITIES AND INTERESTS

Do you enjoy detail work, or would you rather direct the overall project? Do you like to participate in sports, be a spectator, or avoid them completely? Do you prefer stock car races to ballet and opera? Are you creative? Do you like to work with mechanical objects? Numbers? Words? People? All of your abilities and interests are reflected in your personality. And you probably enjoy people with similar preferences.

Our society isn't very accepting of people whose interests differ from the norm. If you prefer health food to pizza and mechanics to golf, then you may not be included in the majority group. You may feel rejected until you find people who share your interests.

Unfortunately, the young don't always have this option. A boy who is not interested in sports has a lonely existence in the neighborhood and at school. In the U.S., the boy who isn't adept with a ball of some kind—football, baseball, or basketball—feels left out; and in Canada, it's the boy who isn't into hockey who feels excluded. In both countries, there are few alternatives to finding a camaraderie with peers, at least until a boy reaches high school.

It's a good idea to expose your children to a variety of activities. And it's not too late to broaden your own interests by trying new things. (See chapter 14 for more on that subject.) Rob, a sports fanatic, agreed to escort his wife to symphony concerts and soon found that he liked them! New endeavors will expand your abilities, widen your circle of friends, and keep you from feeling left out.

BELIEFS AND VALUES

Do you believe in being honest at all costs? In the importance of family life—even if it means cutting back on business hours? Do you value neatness and good care of your personal possessions? What do you believe about God? About environmental issues? About politics? All these beliefs tell people about the real you and affect their responses to you.

Knowing what you believe and constantly living by your values will strengthen your self-esteem. You will gain the respect of others, too, perhaps even those who disagree with you. The exception: If you try too hard to push your views on others, especially those who consider them unreasonable, you will most likely alienate them.

SPIRITUAL GIFTS

Your spiritual gifts are an important part of your personality. Romans 12:6-8 refers to the gifts of prophecy, service, teaching, exhortation, giving, leadership, and mercy. Although we have more than one spiritual gift, we each have a predominant, motivational gift that colors our perspective in every area.

Ignorance of spiritual gifts can cause animosity, envy, even division among Christians. Without an understanding of gifts, we expect others to respond and react just as we do, and we're disappointed with them when they don't. We may say, "I could never do what you're doing," and mean either "I wish I could" or "You must be out of your mind!" A foster parent sheds some light on the problem:

People have often said to us, "I could never do what you're doing." Sometimes they were commending us, but at other times we felt their comment to be an implied criticism. Either way, my silent reaction was usually a holier-than-thou attitude: "You're just making excuses; don't you understand that the children need you, too?"

Then I studied the spiritual gifts and discovered that my basic or motivational gift is probably that of showing mercy. I also learned that one downside of this gift is a tendency to feel critical of those who seem to be less aware of the needs that I see. (Another is a lack of firmness, a tendency to let others take advantage of my willingness to listen and get involved.)

I think we all tend to wear blinders, seeing only our own particular area of concern. I used to feel passionately that every Christian home ought to welcome at least one foster child, and I was impatient that others didn't see the need. I know now that it's the gift of mercy that provides the extra patience needed, not only in that particular work, but in a prison ministry, rescue missions, work with the aged, the profoundly retarded, the terminally ill, and many other ministries to which I give only lip service.

The gift of showing mercy isn't the only motivation behind such ministries; other gifts would be just as usable. But some spiritual gifts are better used in areas of service where I would feel inept and uncomfortable.

It seems that God directs each of us to a special place of service and empowers us with whatever qualities we need to accomplish that work. And it certainly behooves me to be uncritical and accepting and appreciative of those who operate from a different perspective than mine.

Gail shared with us her insight into the gift of mercy and the misunderstanding its use can create:

I have a friend who lets some people walk all over her. I feel they use her without her knowing it. It used to irritate me; it seemed wimpy, and I hated to see her taken advantage of. We even argued the point in a Sunday school class discussion when she said that she couldn't imagine Christ worrying about such a thing; when people needed him, he just responded. She made me feel guilty, which irritated me more, and she admits that she had considered it a spiritual problem when people seemed overly concerned about being taken advantage of.

Now we both understand that our differing thoughts on the subject stem from our differing motivational gifts, and we can appreciate each other's position more. She no longer thinks I am unfeeling or selfish, and I no longer see her as naive and foolish.

An understanding of spiritual gifts can give you insights into your friendships as well:

A friend and I were developing a closer friendship, finding that our common temperament gave us much understanding. Then we began to notice that we were drifting apart. The reason for a lack of common bond became apparent: Her spiritual gift of exhortation causes her to see one-on-one sharing as the most important priority. My gift of administration gives me a broader ministry with a correspondingly tight schedule. We respect one another's gifts, but our vastly different priorities have kept our friendship from attaining the depth we had anticipated. Knowing our gifts has helped us understand why.

We are strongly exhorted in 1 Corinthians 12 to respect the gifts God has given to others. From the least to the greatest, every gift is needed in the body of Christ, just as we need each part of our personal body, from ear to big toe.

My husband and I both have the gift of administration, and we are close friends with another couple who has the gift of giving. A tendency to be organized goes with our gift; it doesn't go with theirs, and we often laugh about that difference. One night while we were visiting at their home, Joe asked Martha where she'd put the bill that had come recently. She thought for a moment and said, "I guess it's under the couch." "Under the couch!" I blurted in disbelief. We all laughed, and I said, "You need a desk." She answered, "We have three, and they're all full!" And we roared, loving each other for our differences.

Understanding one another's spiritual gifts can help us when we work together on boards or committees. In every area of life, it can keep us from judging one another.

ATTITUDE

Others may not relate well to your temperament, your abilities, or your interests, but a positive attitude will attract them to you. Attitude is the aspect of personality that undergirds all the rest. As your outlook becomes more attuned to the positive, you will become more likable and more productive. Performance improves with attitude.

A man who interviews job applicants for his company explained his approach:

Naturally, appearance makes the first impression, but I look for a positive attitude before anything else. Qualifications alone don't make a good employee! I look for people who will fit in. A 4.0 average doesn't mean a thing if the employee doesn't get along with people. One C+ student I hired has climbed higher and faster than anyone else in my department. He contributes, he's productive, he's positive, he's able to mingle, and people respect him. I hire the one with a positive personality instead of the one with a better scholastic record. A negative attitude hampers performance.

A negative outlook will hamper not only your career, but also your friendships. It repels people. A positive attitude, on the other hand, lets you be friendly and caring. But that all-important positiveness is difficult to come by if you sense rejection from others. And that requires, first of all, becoming aware of the pride that stands in the way. Only then can you begin to develop a mind-set that cares about meeting the needs of others.

WHEN PERSONALITIES CLASH

What causes fighting, put-downs, breaches in relationships? Why do we have runaways and divorces? Why are there divisions in every domain, from neighborhoods to conference rooms to churches?

It's because of the nature of pride. Pride, the root of unhealthy self-esteem, says, "You have to be like me in order to be acceptable to me." "If only you would see things my way" is the conscious or subconscious thought running beneath all our conflicts. "My way is better," we think, and another wall goes up in a relationship.

Most people tend to accept people whose personalities are like their own. "I can like you because you are as I am," they reason. "Your beliefs and values resemble mine, we share similar interests, you're on the same social and economic and even intelligence level as I am. So I don't feel inferior or superior to you in any area. You don't intimidate me in any way. I can respect you, and I can feel comfortable with you. Our personalities mesh!"

But every one of us is different from other people in some ways. We are each a unique blend of personality traits. But when we respond negatively to others because of our differences, we encourage unhealthy self-esteem in them. And it comes back to us from them, full circle. Rejection breeds rejection.

PERSONALITY DIFFERENCES IN THE HOME

It is sometimes very difficult to respect the individuality of others—especially at home. We have to live with each other day in and day out, and spending that many hours with a personality that rubs you wrong isn't easy. It takes special effort on your part to maintain a respectful attitude. But the consequences of showing disrespect are significant.

My brother, Brad, is weird; he really bugs me. My sister and I don't think much of him I'm afraid, and neither do our friends. I don't even want other people to know he's my brother. Even my parents have trouble accepting him the way he is.

How healthy do you suppose Brad's self-esteem is? The more he is rejected by his family, the more he will resort to seeking affirmation in unacceptable ways, thus perpetuating a cycle of undesirability and defeat. Someone in that family needs to stop the cycle by assuring Brad through attitude and action that he is a unique person and a valuable member of the family.

The uniqueness that is *you* has been described as butterflies within waiting to be set free. When self-esteem is allowed to struggle free from the cocoon of self-doubt, your personality can open up, freeing the butterflies. But if others don't like your butterflies, you learn to cage them. Your personality is stifled.

The Wilsons are considered to be ideal parents. But in the privacy of home, Dad is dictatorial and critical. Young Jimmy's self-confidence is undermined and he fears rejection. The butterflies of his personality aren't accepted, his uniqueness is caged, and his focus turns inward. If he never feels like a success in some area of his life, his personality may erode into either passivity or anger and aggression. He will become an uninteresting or unlikable adult, and the rejection will continue.

ACCEPTING DIFFERENTNESS

Each of us wants our uniqueness to be respected. Just so, we need to learn to enjoy the uniqueness, the quirks, the off-beat and oddball qualities of others. Those are the things that make us special.

The little comic strip character, Winthrop, once confided: "I think my main problem is that I'm a chocolate ice cream kid living in a broccoli world."

We often assume with Winthrop that we are the ice cream and that others are the broccoli. But that person we look down on is precious to God. He deserves our respect.

"There are no ordinary people," said C. S. Lewis. "You have never talked to a mere mortal!"

It's natural and normal—and even right—for us to seek the shelter of a group of friends with whom we are comfortable because they are much like us. Jesus did so, returning to rest at the home of his friends, Mary, Martha, and Lazarus. But at the same time, he didn't shut out anyone, even those who were considered undesirable. Nor does he indicate that Christians are free to accept only those who are lovable or likable.

Christian friend, if you are only nice to nice people, if you love only those who are lovely, and if you treat the hateful the way they treat you, God's redeeming love is not flowing out from your life.[1]

Scripture repeatedly admonishes us to love, to show forbearance, to be kind.

And so, as those who have been chosen of God, holy and beloved, put on a heart of compassion, kindness, humility, gentleness and patience: bearing with one another, and forgiving each other, whoever has a complaint against any one; just as the Lord forgave you, so also should you. And beyond all these things put on love, which is the perfect bond of unity. (Col. 3:12-14, NASB)

God gave us our unique personalities, each so different, yet so interdependent. But regardless of our personality, every one of us needs to feel accepted and acceptable. The need is intense, perhaps overriding everything else. For that reason, when you communicate acceptance and affirmation to others, you are more apt to be liked and appreciated. Perhaps as with Miss Evans, others will even see you as beautiful!

God says, "Humble yourselves therefore under the mighty hand of God, that he may exalt you in due time" (1 Pet. 5:6, KJV). But the world says, "Exalt yourself! Keep your focus on yourself! Look out for number one! Me first!" The message around us is simple and virulent: The way to *be* first is to be beautiful and intelligent, to have the right personality, the right position, and the money to make it all happen. And we listen.

We're gullible. We've been indoctrinated with false and shifting values. We're swept along by an increasingly feelings-oriented culture. Feelings begin to transcend facts. But we need something more reliable, something true for a measuring stick. Our thinking patterns need an overhaul. We need to shake ourselves loose from the values around us. We need a deliberate mind-set focused on what really matters!

What really matters is your position in Christ.

. . . Behold, a voice spoke from heaven, a still, small voice, and it said, ". . . You have exalted what I have not promised. . . . When have I promised you . . . earthly comfort? When have I promised you continued possession of beauty, intelligence, or virtue? When have I told you that in this world humankind will always know justice and peace? . . . When have I promised an easy lot for the sons of men, even the Christian sons of men?" . . .

Then, O Lord, what will you give us?

And the voice replied, "Myself."

We may have health, we may have friends, we may have justice, but all we are sure of is God. . . . God gives to us Himself. And this is all that counts. . . .[2]

Beauty, intelligence, a likable personality, great wealth—each is subject to change with the passage of time or change of circumstances. All you can be sure of is God. Your position in Christ matters most.

Can you accept God's approval and focus your attention on his values? If you can, you will be less vulnerable to unhealthy self-esteem. You may even develop immunity.

QUESTIONS FOR PERSONAL APPLICATION

1. What attracts you to other people?
2. Think of someone you consider to have a great personality. What is it about him that makes you feel that way?
3. If you do not know the predominant temperament types of your family members, consider reading a book on the subject so you will be better equipped to understand and accept them.
4. List some new activities you and your family might explore. In what ways might these bring benefit?
5. How would knowing and living by what you believe strengthen your self-esteem?
6. Can you think of instances in which your irritation with a person stemmed from a lack of understanding or acceptance of a spiritual gift different from yours?
7. Do you think people would rate your attitude as being positive? If not, what is it that keeps you from being that way? How would your

family benefit if you were to strive for a more positive attitude? How will you cultivate a positive self-attitude?

8. How do you react to someone who is criticizing one of his own family members?

9. Does your attitude toward your children free their personalities or cage them? Is one child's personality less acceptable to you than another's? Why? Does your spouse feel you are accepting of him or her?

10. If you regard someone in your family as an oddity, answer question 7 in Questions for Group Discussion.

11. List the values that should be important to a Christian. How can you set your mind on those values the next time you're feeling down?

12. What is temporal about your life? What is eternal about your life? Do your priorities show which is most important to you?

QUESTIONS FOR GROUP DISCUSSION

1. Consider how different temperaments could cause misunderstanding and friction in a home or church.

2. Discuss why others will respect you for living out your beliefs. What behaviors or beliefs might bring alienation?

3. Answer question 5 in Questions for Personal Application.

4. How might differing spiritual gifts cause misunderstanding and friction?

5. Discuss in what ways a positive outlook would be an asset in a job and at home. How can we cultivate a positive attitude?

6. Discuss what it means to cage the "butterflies" of someone's personality.

7. Suppose Brad were *your* brother or child. How do you think he feels about all the rejection in his life? What facades might he be wearing? What would improve your attitude toward him? How would you communicate your new acceptance to him?

8. Answer question 8 in Questions for Personal Application.

9. What did C. S. Lewis mean when he said, "There are no ordinary people. You have never talked to a mere mortal"?

10. How do we communicate acceptance and affirmation? How can we become more alert to opportunities to do this?

11. How do you think you would cope with the loss of beauty, intelligence, personality, wealth, or worldly success?

12. If you could change one thing about yourself, which would you choose: looks, intelligence, socioeconomic status, or personality? How do you think that change would affect your life?

nurturing healthy self-esteem

8   The Underlying Disease
The Origins of Pride

Can you imagine life without any painful memories of put-downs? Without feelings of inadequacy because of past failures? Without the lingering sting of embarrassing moments? Without the urge to withdraw into self-pity or hostile silence?

That's what life was like for Adam and Eve in those blissful early days of creation. Adam didn't feel hounded by a nagging wife, and Eve didn't feel threatened by a domineering husband. There were no in-law problems or office rivalries. The couple didn't fight about how much Eve spent at the Garden Style Shoppe or how soon Adam was going to fix things around the house. Their marriage relationship didn't suffer from

- put-downs,
- outbursts of temper,
- disrespect,
- irritation,
- stubbornness,
- power struggles.

Why? Because they had no feelings of superiority or inferiority. Each of them had a perfectly healthy self-esteem. Self-centeredness hadn't entered their lives, so they were free to enjoy God and each other.

THE BIRTH OF SELF-CONCERN

What introduced self-centeredness, with all its hurtful by-products? The tragedy is told with simplicity in the third chapter of Genesis. It is a short story, but it changed all of humanity from that time on.

Satan wanted Adam and Eve to follow him; it was as simple as that. Pride had toppled him from God's kingdom, and he knew it would do the same for them. How could he transmit the infection to accomplish his purpose? Perhaps he could persuade Eve to doubt what God had said and then to rationalize her disobedience. "Hey, Eve," he whispered, "if you follow my suggestion you'll become wise like God! What could be wrong with that?"

And it worked! It made sense to Eve, and the fruit was tempting. She persuaded Adam to join her, and as they ate, their disobedience brought sin to all mankind.

All sin can be traced to the root of self-centeredness—the same basis for the temptation in the Garden. Adam and Eve yielded to the seduction because they saw that the fruit was good for food, a delight to the eyes, and desirable to make them wise (Gen. 3:6, NASB). These same temptations have been translated throughout all history as the lust of the flesh, the lust of the eyes, and the boastful pride of life (1 John 2:16, NASB).

The Amplified Bible speaks of these temptations in familiar terms: cravings for sensual gratification, greedy longings of the mind, and confidence in our own resources and in the stability of earthly things. How apt a description of our world's false values!

With their attention riveted on their lustful desires and their own knowledge, Adam and Eve became centered on themselves for the first time in their lives. Humanity's consuming self-concern was born.

BY-PRODUCTS OF SELFISHNESS

What a change this new self-focus must have brought in the relationship of that first couple! Suddenly they found themselves angry, hurt, critical of each other, and prone to self-pity and hostile silences. How bewildering! Perhaps they were even frightened—and certainly frustrated—as these unfamiliar emotions and reactions surfaced. Adam and Eve had begun to experience the breach in relationships that has been normal ever since.

The rest of Scripture is a sad commentary on the selfish nature of humanity. The children of Israel repeatedly complained, grumbled, and disobeyed. Even the most respected, godly leaders of the Old Testament had problems rooted in self-centeredness:

- *Pride* provoked Moses to disobey God and forfeit his entrance into the Promised Land.
- *Lust of the eyes* led David to take another man's wife and arrange for the death of her husband.
- *Lust of the flesh* resulted in the downfall of Solomon and Samson.

Even Jesus' disciples suffered from self-centeredness. Twice, as Jesus was walking with them, he told them of his coming death and resurrection, but they didn't understand what he meant; they were preoccupied with assessing who was greatest among them (Mark 9:31-34; 10:33-37).

Selfishness rears its ugly head all around us. Its extremes are manifested in terrorism, military aggression, murder, rape, and all manner of abusive behavior.

Society is destroying itself with its insatiable lusts. People crave illegitimate sex, excess food, alcohol, drugs, and power. Most of us are more interested in getting what our eyes lust after—someone else's mate, more things, whatever looks good to us—than in meeting the needs of others. We'll go to almost any lengths to prove our desires are right. And the effect of our behavior on mates, children, or parents hardly matters as long as we get our way.

The drive to protect pride is incredibly strong. We are ever the defenders, and we constantly look for reinforcement from others. Unfortunately, other people are just as concerned about defending *their* pride, no matter what the cost may be to *you*.

Who were you concerned about when you were taunted by a classmate at recess? Who becomes the focus of your thoughts when you are criticized? The same person whose face you probably look for first in a group snapshot. And so with every blow to your ego, you become more focused on yourself.

Satan's plan was ingenious and certainly successful: Fill people with pride, and their allegiance would be his forever. Rather than respond to God, people would perpetuate their self-centeredness. They would alternately be inflated with conceit and deflated by feelings of inferiority. And they would be pawns in Satan's hands.

Satan delights in hindering your fellowship with God. When Adam and Eve disobeyed him, not only did their relationship with each other change drastically, but their relationship with God was forever altered. They had known total openness with him, but now their sin brought a separation—for them and for all mankind to follow.

THE PERFECT CURE FOR THE SELF SYNDROME

The effects of pride were no surprise to God, and he had the solution. When the time was right, and generation after generation had proved that perfect goodness was beyond its reach, he would provide the cure: his righteousness put into man.

God's actions are incomprehensible to the human mind! God, in Christ,

- came into the world,
- took on the body of a man,
- died on a cross to pay the price our sin required,
- rose again in complete victory over death,
- gave us the sure hope of resurrected life.

Our goodness is as filthy rags before God (Isa. 64:6). But he offers us salvation (and his righteousness) as a free gift (Rom. 6:23)!

God has provided the perfect cure for our sinful nature. So why is the disease of self-centeredness still so prevalent? Because medicine doesn't cure until it is taken, and our prideful nature insists we don't need God's cure—or, at the other extreme, that we don't deserve it.

Some people believe that church membership and good deeds will please God; they don't need a Savior. Others think they are too unworthy to be acceptable to God. Either way, Satan has kept people focused on their own strengths or weaknesses

- so they won't realize that Christ has earned God's forgiveness for them,
- so they won't claim it for themselves,
- so they won't ask God to apply it to their lives.

Your nature of sin came from Satan, so you can never succeed in overcoming it yourself. *The sin nature came from someone beyond you, and it takes Someone beyond you to overcome it!* You need only to accept God's cure.

Satan tempted Adam and Eve in order to bring them under his authority, and he'll not easily surrender anyone to God. He is the master deceiver. He does his job so well that if a random survey were taken in your city asking people what it means to be a Christian, most would answer that a Christian is a person who goes to church and lives a decent life. Others would a say a Christian is one who has been baptized and takes communion on a regular basis. "God will accept me if the good in my life outweighs the bad," they reason.

What does the Bible say? That a Christian is one who understands that he is a sinner and needs the Savior because he cannot meet God's standard of perfection. Consequently, he has asked God to apply Christ's death and resurrection to his life (Rom. 3:19-24).

THE BENEFITS OF BELIEF

What will salvation do for a battered self-esteem?

As you come to Christ, you will find a new focus of life—God rather than yourself. With such a stable center, you will no longer need to vacillate between feelings of superiority and inferiority.

- Pride in your own goodness is laid aside;
- God's forgiveness removes your guilt;
- Your sense of worthlessness is replaced by God's valued opinion of you.

In God's sight, each person stands at the same place of leveling—the foot of the cross. You now learn to see others as God sees them—equal before him.

I don't need forgiveness. (I'm good enough.)
I don't deserve forgiveness. (I'm too unworthy.)
I am forgiven. (I have worth as God's child.)

Since the Fall we have had to derive our self-esteem from interaction with other fallen people. As a result, we will never have self-esteem as Adam and Eve had—based not on other people, but on God. We'll never know complete freedom from self-centeredness and painful memories of past hurts—at least in this life. But as believers in Christ, God has provided:

- the comfort of his unconditional love,
- the peace of his complete forgiveness,
- the leadership and instruction of his Spirit.

And one day we'll be free from blows and hurts and self-centeredness, free to live in God's presence in perfect harmony with him and with others. In heaven, we will be completely cured of all unhealthy self-esteem!

In the meantime, we have one perfect example of healthy self-esteem—the Son of God, Jesus Christ, who knew who he was and why he was here. He didn't cling to a position of superiority. He willingly surrendered every normal earthly right that would interfere with his task. He didn't demand a home, a bed, three square meals a day, or a family to give him security and prestige. He didn't struggle to defend his honor or protect his pride. And we know the result. "Therefore also God highly exalted Him . . ." (Phil. 2:9, NASB). Because he accepted servanthood, God magnified him. What a model for us to follow!

QUESTIONS FOR PERSONAL APPLICATION

1. In what way does the "lust of the flesh" tempt you? The "lust of the eyes"? Pride in your own resources? How might you overcome these temptations? Be specific.
2. Do you often insist your way is right or better? How can you change that attitude?
3. What kinds of people or circumstances tend to trigger a defensive reaction within you? Does this ever cause you to lose control? What specific steps can you take to change? It took a long time to cement your habits, and it may take a long time before change is consistent. Keep a record until you see victories outnumber defeats.
4. Is there anyone you have hurt through defensive behavior? In what ways? How will you change? Will you ask for forgiveness?
5. The next time you are criticizing someone, even justifiably, stop and consider your root motive. Does it stem from a sense of superiority? Or perhaps a need to bolster your self-esteem?
6. When feelings of inferiority begin to overtake you, how might you avoid a pity party? How can you get your focus off yourself and onto God's values and others' needs instead?

7. What does it mean to you to be a Christian? (Read Rom. 3:23; 5:8; 6:23; Eph. 2:8-9; John 1:12.) Have you applied these verses to your life and received Jesus Christ as your Savior? If you have, what does 1 John 5:13 promise you? John 5:24?
8. Does self-centeredness still need to be dealt with in your life, even though you have received Jesus as Savior?
9. Apply Jesus' example of selflessness to your own life. What rights are you willing to surrender in order to meet the needs of others?

QUESTIONS FOR GROUP DISCUSSION

1. Discuss what life might have been like for Adam and Eve before self-centeredness entered their lives. How would it differ from life as we know it today?
2. How can poor self-esteem lead to marital problems?
3. Can you think of any sins that aren't rooted in self-centeredness?
4. In what ways do we protect our pride? How might we hurt others in the process?
5. How can we express helpful criticism without being drawn into a superior attitude?
6. Why is it easier to detect feelings of inferiority in yourself than to recognize a superior attitude?
7. Discuss how Jesus' example of selflessness might be applied to our lives. What rights might we need to be willing to surrender in order to meet the needs of others?
8. How might we help our children become more aware of the needs of others?
9. If our goodness isn't good enough for God, what is?
10. Select prayer partners. What one area of change do you want to be held accountable for this week?

9 The Father's Antidote
The Power of Unconditional Love

A young mother wrote us this note:

*I grew up hating myself. My low self-esteem controlled me.
After committing my life to Christ, I recognized that from
God's point of view I am very important and unique, and I am
made worthy through Christ. But I don't know how to use this
new knowledge to refocus and repair my poor self-esteem. I
don't know how to alter my thought patterns.*

If a person fails to receive love as a child, he may have
difficulty understanding the nature of love as an adult.
Sandy, who was once in foster care, says with pathos:

*It doesn't matter if a child is five or thirty-five, being unloved
by your parents hurts! I feel quite unlovable. I keep trying to
convince myself that I'm a good person. I ask my husband,
"Why do you love me?" He says he can't explain it; he just
loves me for who I am. I cannot comprehend this. I can under-
stand why other people are loved. But not me. I honestly feel I
have little redeeming social value. I can understand how God
loves us all because his heart is pure, his love is limitless, his*

understanding perfect. But people have limits. People need
reasons. People like perfection. Please keep praying for me,
that someday I'll feel good about myself.

The communication of love is perhaps 90 percent nonver-
bal; *attitude* is more important than words. The tone of
voice, the expression on a face, a touch, a look, can all say,
"I love you"—or the opposite! It's possible to give 10 per-
cent affirmation by *saying,* "I love you," while communi-
cating with the other 90 percent, "I don't really mean it."
That's not only confusing; it is painful, even devastating.

Skin hunger—the need to be touched, the need to be
hugged—is universal and well-documented.

Two fourteen-year-old girls were temporary foster placements
in our home, and sometimes I found it difficult to get any work
accomplished; it seemed one or the other always had her arms
around me.

One day as I was preparing for dinner, Julie came looking
for a hug, and my silent reaction as her arms went around my
waist was "Oh, no, not again." But the feeling was momentary.
As I turned from the stove to respond, Susan came up behind us
and said, "You know why we like to hug you all the time?
Because it's so nice to be hugged back!"

"Yeah," said Julie, "my mom gets mad when I hug her."

Susan nodded. "My mom yells, 'Can't you see I'm busy?' "
She paused, then said softly, "It's really nice to be hugged
back."

And we stood there in a three-way embrace while the
potatoes boiled over.

THREE KINDS OF LOVE

If hugs or other nonverbal expressions of love were withheld
during your growing years, you may have an incomplete
view of love as an adult. Many times the love we receive as
children is based on performance. It's common to think all

love parallels what we were given at home. As a result, you may conclude that your marriage partner and your friends love you only when you perform acceptably or impressively. You may think that God's love is equally conditional. "My parents don't even like me and I can't stand myself. He's a holy God. How could he love *me?*" asks one young woman. Doubt and longing exude from that painful question. It is repeated by many.

There are different kinds of love, you know. We are all familiar with *if* love. *Because* love is common. But *anyhow* love is hard to find and seldom experienced.

If love says, "If you scratch my back, I'll scratch yours." *Because* love says, "Because you love me, or please me, or perform as I wish, I am able to love you." *Anyhow* love says, "It's all right; I accept you and love you anyhow."

Ten-year-old Ronnie had been living in our home for a few weeks when I commited some foolish faux pas to the glee of my teenagers, who began hooting in fun, enjoying my ineptitude as well as my embarrassment. Ronnie looked on, watching my face uncertainly. Suddenly he darted across the room, threw his arms around my waist, and defied my tormentors, declaring, "Well, I love her!"

Ronnie didn't care how foolish or inept or inadequate I might be; he loved me anyhow.

The Bible talks about *anyhow* love in Romans 5:8: "But God demonstrates his own love for us in this: While we were still sinners, Christ died for us" (NIV). It repeats the theme in 1 John 4:10: "This is love: not that we loved God, but that he loved us and sent his Son as an atoning sacrifice for our sins" (NIV). Another picture appears in Jeremiah 31:3: "I have loved you with an everlasting love; therefore I have drawn you with lovingkindness" (NASB).

Notice there is no "if," "because," or "but" in any of the statements. God isn't saying you must get your act together before he will accept you. He isn't telling you to straighten up and fly right so he'll be able to love you. His everlasting love is the *anyhow* kind. He says, "It's all right; I love you anyhow." Not that your sin doesn't matter. It *does* matter—it sent Christ to the cross. But he loves you anyhow!

HOW GOD SEES YOU

Do you still ask, "But how can God love me?" Perhaps you are sometimes deeply thankful that people don't know the real you—thankful that others can't see all those thoughts and feelings and attitudes you try to keep hidden. Yet God knows you more thoroughly than you know yourself (Ps. 139). He even knows things about you that you don't want to know. And still he accepts and loves you.

That isn't all. If you have asked God to apply Christ's death and resurrection to your life, you are

- his blameless one (Eph. 1:4),
- his chosen one, in whom he delights (Eph. 1:4, 11; Ps. 37:23),
- his heir and his adopted child (Eph. 1:5).

NOTE: *Adopted* is a crucial word. Everyone is not automatically included in the family of God. Even the finest people are not inherently his children (See Rom. 8:14; Eph. 2:19; John 8:42, 47.) All humankind is God's creation, so the brotherhood of man is valid to that extent. But Scripture repeatedly refers to our *adoption* as his children when we, by an act of the will, open the door of our lives and *receive* Jesus Christ (Eph. 1:5; Gal. 4:5). "But as many as received Him, to them He gave the right to *become* the children of God, even to those who believe in his name" (John 1:12, NASB, emphasis added).

You are very special to God—special enough for Jesus Christ to leave the glories of heaven and come to this earth, live as mortal man, and suffer utter, incomprehensible anguish. He came just to take your sin on himself and to make you acceptable to God (1 Pet. 2:24; 3:18). His actions should answer once and for all the question that is so central to self-esteem: "How much am I worth?"

Friends may withdraw from you if you fail them again and again. But Christ says in John 5:24 that if you are trusting in him you will never come under judgment when you fail; you have already passed out of death and into eternal life. Bad, selfish, and rebellious you may well be. He loves and accepts you anyhow—unconditionally.

But the tempter tries to confuse us, and his deception can be broad and blatant — or specific and subtle. This young man's experience is common in the Christian community:

I returned home from a week at Bible camp and told my Christian parents that I had asked Christ into my life the night before. My parents were soft-spoken, low-key people not given to outward displays of temper, and occasionally, when my attitude was especially bad, Mother would pin me down with a quiet, "I thought you were a Christian now." Sometimes she added, "You certainly aren't acting like one!" So I often questioned my experience. Now an adult, I know my place in God's family, but even yet, doubts plague me when I blunder in my relationships or fail to live up to what I think God expects of me.

Of course, unconfessed sin will erect a barrier in our relationship with Christ, hurting not his view of us, but our fellowship with him. With that in mind, we need to be careful to do the following:

- recognize our sin,
- confess it,
- thank God for the forgiveness he has already provided.

Isn't it beautiful that salvation is a free gift that doesn't have to be earned by following a set of rules? Isn't it comforting that God knows how susceptible you are to temptation and *provides for your forgiveness?* You could never pay for your sins by being good enough, so he *has done it for you!*

Because of his kindness you have been saved through trusting Christ. And even trusting is not of yourselves; it too is a gift from God. Salvation is not a reward for the good you have done, so none of us can take any credit for it. (Eph. 2:8-9, TLB)

THE CURE FOR UNHEALTHY SELF-ESTEEM

If you understand how God sees you, if you believe he knows you inside and out—the good, the bad, and the indifferent—and still loves you, then you will be able to agree with him that what he created is good. He didn't make any mistakes with you. "God don't make no junk!"

But it's not that easy, is it? Theological fact struggles with harsh reality. We may know all the biblical answers, but we have trouble when it comes to applying them to a shaky self-concept in everyday life. How can we build our self-esteem on a firm foundation?

When you ask God to apply Christ's death to your life, you can take the first step toward strong, healthy self-esteem. If you trust in Jesus Christ and believe that God's Word is absolutely true, you can *know* that he accepts you unconditionally (John 5:24; Rom. 5:1; 8:1). Even though you may often grieve him, you can accept yourself as he accepts you. You can be glad to be you!

As you begin to understand how special you are to God, you see that everyone else is special too. The handicapped man, the deformed child, the slow learner, even the person you find most unappealing and unlikable—all are just as special to the Father as you and those who are dear to you.

If people are made in the image of God, then some of his image is present in everyone you know. When you let God begin to change your self-centered nature, more of his image will be seen in you. And you will be able to help others do the same.

QUESTIONS FOR PERSONAL APPLICATION

1. How do you communicate love through your body language?
2. Why is your nonverbal communication of love more believable than your words?
3. In what other creative ways could you express love to your family and friends?
4. How can you tell if your love for someone is the *if,* the *because,* or the *anyhow* kind?
5. For whom could you express *anyhow* love?
6. Of all the people you know, who do you feel has best learned *anyhow* love? What makes you think so?
7. If the love you received as a child was conditional (*if* or *because* love), do you think it has hampered your ability to give or receive *anyhow* love? How can you overcome that handicap?
8. How will the knowledge that God knows you fully yet loves you anyhow affect your relationships with people?
9. Though God loves you with *anyhow* love, he expects you to obey him. Have you been hanging on to some sin because you know God will love you anyway? Apply 1 John 1:9 to all known sin in your life.
10. Do you believe God when he says he delights in you and loves you? Begin thanking him and believing him today!

QUESTIONS FOR GROUP DISCUSSION

1. Brainstorm ways we communicate love through body language alone.
2. Discuss question 2 in Questions for Personal Application.
3. Brainstorm other means of saying "I love you."
4. Give some examples of *if* love, *because* love, and *anyhow* love.
5. Which kind of love do we most often see demonstrated? Why do you think that is?
6. Discuss question 7 from Questions for Personal Application.
7. Discuss question 8 from Questions for Personal Application.
8. Why can't a person become a Christian by following the Golden Rule?
9. Select prayer partners for this week. Pray that each member of the group will have the opportunity and the grace to demonstrate *anyhow* love.

10   Placebos Don't Cure
How We Cope with Emotional Pain

"Only dull people have immaculate houses!" That line would be hard to prove, but I like it. I cut it out of a women's magazine so many years ago that the clipping eventually fell apart. But I pasted it onto a piece of cardboard, and when that began to wear out I copied it on to a three-by-five card. It still occupies a prominent place on my bulletin board. I still like it. I guess I need it.

Even in such mundane activity as housework, the need to bolster our ego is always present. So we sometimes say things like:

- "Their house is beautiful, but it doesn't look lived-in; it's too perfect."
- "Their home could be lovely, but . . . ."
- "I know she's a busy person, but . . . ."
- "I don't understand how they can spend so much on furniture (or cars, or gadgets); my conscience wouldn't let me."
- "If we had the kind of breaks they've had . . . ."

What you're really saying through comments like these is that you are just as good as "they" are or "she" is—or maybe a little better. At least *you* have your priorities straight.

But if you *did* have your priorities straight, you'd consider what it's like walking in the other person's shoes. You would make allowances for her shortcomings and appreciate her strengths. Instead, because pride is the predominant force in life, you may look for some way to provide good feelings about yourself—even at the expense of another.

Putting others down is a universal method of building oneself up. *Everyone* uses it, judging others silently or vocally. But it's only one of many strategies. When self-esteem has been badly trampled, defensive or protective coping can come packaged as arrogance, anger, hostility, or apparent indifference.

Teddy, for example, is cocky, loud, overbearing, opinionated, difficult to like. Who understands that he is just desperately trying to hide his insecurity—even from himself? For Teddy, acting superior is such an effective relief from the pain of rejection he felt at home that it has become a way of life. Feeling unwanted, or living with criticism and harshness, leaves wounds that don't heal easily.

We all hide behind other faces when our self-esteem is attacked. Sometimes we avoid acknowledging the blows. A child who lives with rebuffs from peers may try to hide the fact from his parents for fear they will think less of him, too. For the same reason, he won't want teachers and peers to know about problems he experiences at home.

Other times we mask our feelings, pretending we don't hurt while at the same time groping for an aspirin. And many times what we grasp for so desperately is only a placebo.

Placebos and analgesics come in many forms. Some are more effective cover-ups than others, and some might even dull the pain for a while. Dr. James Dobson suggests six basic coping patterns that are familiar to counselors: I'll be a clown, I'll withdraw, I'll fight, I'll deny reality, I'll conform, I'll compensate.[1] We need to recognize these various methods of coping to understand what is behind our actions and reactions. Why do you do what you do and feel what you feel and say what you say? Are you basically

- a comedian,
- a withdrawer,
- an attacker,
- an escapist,
- a conformist—

or have you learned to compensate and be open to change?

COMEDY

Every comedian isn't necessarily covering up a poor self-esteem, but turning to comedy is just one of the many tools we use to hide our inadequacies. Art Buchwald says he had to do something because he wasn't athletic, and the only thing he could do was be funny. The "schlemiel mentality" was explored by *Newsweek* in a study of the childhoods of forty-three well-known comics of past and present. Most seemed to fit the pattern: "clumsy misfits . . . troubled youngsters . . . behavior problems . . . poor performers in school. . . . In general, each had been an irritation to teachers and parents."[2]

Loneliness and rejection seem to characterize the child-hoods of many top comedians. According to *Parade*, Rodney Dangerfield began to write comedy routines as a teenager to escape feelings of loneliness. Said Dangerfield:

I'm a serious guy, not a real clown. . . . Jack Benny once told me that I had the perfect thing. His thing was that he was supposed to be thirty-nine and stingy. But my image, he said, touched the soul of everybody. Old or young, black or white, everyone thinks he's a loser in life.[3]

Bette Midler told interviewer Gene Shalit:

I had a rough time when I was in elementary school and junior high, but by the time I got to high school I figured out how to be the toast of the school. I was just very funny. Do you realize how many sad or unhappy people have turned to comedy in early childhood?[4]

A comedian with an unhealthy self-esteem will make a joke of everything to deny or, at least, conceal his sense of not measuring up to others. He even learns to laugh with others at himself. Their delighted response feeds his ego and puts a lid on the hurt, and for a while he's on top of the world. The aspirin is somewhat effective in alleviating the pain, *but not in curing the illness.*

WITHDRAWAL

Karen copes by withdrawing. She took a different route than the comedian and grew a hedge around herself. She became self-insulated.

Withdrawing is her defense against never getting as many valentines as her schoolmates, against not being invited to their birthday parties, against not being included in their jokes, against being laughed at in gym class. No matter what your age, if you feel excluded from the in-group because you don't measure up to its standards, it hurts. Withdrawal is one insulation against more rejection.

Karen, for example, hesitates to speak unless she is first spoken to. She feels grateful appreciation if she is noticed and acknowledged by a more popular classmate in the halls or in class. She usually eats lunch alone. (A noisy, crowded school cafeteria can be the loneliest place in the world!) Since she won't intrude on a group engaged in conversation or press an opinion unless she's directly asked, shy, intelligent Karen is often dismissed as being snobbish or dull.

Dr. Dobson finds that withdrawers "are in a high-risk

group for ulcers, migraine headaches, acute colitis, and other psychosomatic illnesses. . . . As housewives, they live with depression . . . leading them down the road to secret alcoholism. A husband with the same response to his problems may become a henpecked Milquetoast. Since he lacks the ego strength to lead the family, he must be content to follow in silence."[5]

If you are a self-insulator, your inferiority complex may be severe. And severely painful. You *know* that others consider you inferior. So you are careful not to call attention to yourself in any way; you keep to yourself when you are away from the safety of home. In childhood, you may have been so cooperative and eager to please, especially at school, that your symptoms were overlooked. Many people are naturally reserved and quiet, but if you cope with feelings of inferiority, you will never find permanent relief. Withdrawal is not only stressful, but also dangerous because it tends to mask the illness. You continue to suffer in silence.

ATTACK
Sometimes the pain caused by frequent withdrawal pushes a person into the opposite aisle. By attacking others, he can rise immediately above a sense of inferiority—for a time, at least.

A person who responds to others aggressively may be supersensitive and self-protective, imagining slights where none are intended. He is easily angered and his most useful weapon is sarcasm. He needs to retaliate in some way, any way. He feels justified in his attacks, having no concern for the pain—even permanent damage—he may be inflicting; he suffers from total self-focus. He insists on being right; he'd feel threatened if he were forced to concede a point in an argument or discussion. In fact, failure to agree with him is taken as a personal affront; he is quick to take offense.

Blows to the attacker's pride are quickly deflected by a facade of superiority, so it may come as a surprise to his victims, and even to himself, that his attacks are simply reactions to his poor self-esteem. That's his way of coping, his placebo.

The attacker needs much affirmation, but no one offers it because he seems to think so much of himself already. The long-suffering wife of one such person objected, "No way am I going to find things to praise him for! He already thinks he's perfect." But she is so wrong. Regular affirmation just might begin to soften his abrasive personality.

ESCAPE

Denying reality is an equally nonproductive way to cope with unhealthy self-esteem. Denial of reality can induce a psychotic state of mind that deals with problems by pretending they don't exist. More commonly, people employ escape tactics by simply denying they have a problem. They refuse to face their need. In this way, problems continue to build up without resolution.

You may sometimes indulge in another escape mechanism common to lonely withdrawers: creating a dream world that can take over whenever your mind is otherwise unoccupied. By dreaming you can shut out reality but still return to the real world upon demand. In your dreams you can be everything you wish to be—someone you feel good about. You can create a pseudo self-worth. Movies, books, television, and other means will transport you into this dream world. It can become an addiction. Constantly escaping into a dream world is unsuitable and dangerous for the Christian. Satan will exploit a passive state of mind to the fullest extent.

Real escapers often are alcohol and drug abusers from unstable, unhappy, or uncaring homes. It's a big, cold world out there if you have no one to fall back on, no one who really cares what happens in your life. The future can look bleak and depressing, and sometimes it seems the only alternative is to blot it out for a while.

But alcohol and drugs are like the hypodermic injection one receives before being wheeled into the operating room—an anesthetic used to dull reality. They may offer a temporary escape from a painful world, but the escape hatch can quickly turn into a trap of anguish.

Your circumstances may seem too difficult to face. Choosing to be honest with yourself may require much courage but its benefits make it worth the effort. One participant in our self-esteem class wrote us:

I went home from the first two sessions devastated. I recognized I'd been escaping into a dream world, denying reality, pretending everything was all right, refusing to face facts. And I'd been living that way for years.

You forced me to face reality and it was very painful. There's a lot of guilt to face up to. But God began his healing work, and he's changing me.

CONFORMITY

The desire to feel comfortable by fitting in with other people is a universal need. Our tendency to conform to those around us can lead to positive patterns of behavior, such as church attendance, or negative patterns of behavior that can create harmful dependency.

For example, "everybody" takes a social drink now and then, and cocktail parties are an important part of the business and social scene. Nobody wants to be a Goody-Two-Shoes or a Nice Nelly. So we succumb to the pressures of the crowd—in spite of the fact that alcoholism is often identified as the number one disease of our society.

What are the results of our conformity? Battered families and highway carnage testify to the virulence of intoxication. Drug and alcohol abuse touch almost every home in America in some way. Teenagers, and even children, are hooked on alcohol in increasing numbers. A report published in 1977 by the U.S. Department of Housing, Education, and Welfare claimed that more than 9 million children *under the age of fourteen* drank enough to be considered moderate drinkers! And this figure has escalated every year since.

Yet with the horrifying statistics before us, alcohol continues to be accepted and used by parents who want to be a part of *their* crowd. Teenage drinking seems to be clearly related to parental habits as well as to peer pressure. Teenagers are under heavy pressure to conform; their parents face the same need of acceptance. No matter what your age, if you feel unsure of your place in the world, you will adapt to prevailing opinion and custom in order to feel acceptable.

The influence of peer pressure is especially strong in junior high school, when a child's self-esteem is vulnerable. Carry an umbrella? Wear a hat? "Motherrrrrrr!" your child responds, which means, "Nobody else does."

When she was in junior and senior high, our daughter was described as always looking like a doll that just stepped out of the box. Then she entered college, and sometimes we were ashamed to claim her! Suddenly the only requirements were warmth and comfort. "Anything goes"—that was conformity on the campus in the early 1970s.

Peer pressure has such a tremendous influence on self-esteem that countless adolescents enter into sexual relationships because "Boys expect it" or "Girls expect it." Movies, television, and popular music all assure them it's the norm. *Newsweek* reported:

Many teenagers are having sex as much because it is available and fashionable as because it is desirable. . . . There is more pressure than ever. . . . While adolescents are traditionally rebellious, within their own circles they tend to be fiercely conformist. . . . Among teenagers, peer pressure is one of the most important reasons for taking the sexual plunge. . . . A fifteen-year-old says, "It was totally against what I was, but it was important to be a part of a group. Everybody was having sex. . . ." One sixteen-year-old summed it up: "It must have been a lot easier when society set the standards for you. It can get awfully complicated. I guess that's the price we have to pay for freedom."[6]

What a sad commentary! Freedom from parental rules can bring enslavement to the mores of the group. Even as adults, we accept, submit, and comply to the standards of the crowd because it is so important to feel included.

A word of caution: Be careful about attributing self-esteem problems to a person whose behavior fits one of the preceding patterns. Some conformity is essential for civilized living, and everyone escapes into daydreaming sometimes. The phlegmatic or the introvert may not be coping by withdrawing, he may be just naturally quiet. And some fortunate extroverts are spontaneously funny, with a delightful wit and a sunny disposition to match—a joy to know and to live with. *A quick wit or a reserved personality do not necessarily indicate unhealthy self-esteem!*
But when one or more of these behaviors is overused to cope with unhealthy self-esteem, it is helpful to know better methods of response.

COMPENSATION
The trouble with placebos and analgesics is that they don't cure the illness. Most methods of coping with unhealthy self-esteem give only a temporary lift, a facade of health. Compensation, in contrast, can create valid good feelings about yourself and a lasting, realistic lift.
Compensation involves making up for real or imagined deficiencies by concentrating on one's strengths and developing new skills. Sometimes compensation can be negative—buying sprees and eating binges, for instance—but let's concentrate on its positive aspects. An advice columnist shared this letter:

Dear Abby,
A year ago I was a poor student, shy, lonely, friendless, un-
happy, and I never smiled. I wrote to you, and you gave me the
best advice I ever received. Here it is:

"The key to being popular with both sexes is: Be kind. Be
honest. Be tactful. If you can't be beautiful (or handsome), be
well-groomed, tastefully attired, trim of figure, and Keep a
Smile on Your Face!

"Be clean in body and mind. If you're not a 'brain,' try
harder. If you're not a great athlete, you can be a good sport.
Try to be a standout in something. If you can't dance or sing,
learn to play an instrument. Think for yourself, but respect the
rules. Be generous with kind words and affectionate gestures,
but save the heavy artillery for later. You'll be glad you did. If
you need help, ask God. If you don't need anything, thank God.
Love, Abby"

I followed your advice step-by-step, and kept it handy when I
felt low. I am now president of the sophomore class, and I play
the guitar. Smiling comes naturally to me, and I have a boy-
friend who is kind and respectable. My grades are better, and I
have more friends now than I ever dreamed I'd have. Abby,
you're not the only one who helped me. God helped me. He
answered my prayers.

Carol[7]

Compensation also means using painful experiences
constructively. Many times we can learn valuable lessons
and see positive results following a negative experience.

My socially difficult school years gave me an empathy that
now helps me communicate with teenagers. I recognize the
isolation and loneliness that accompany a sense of social
inadequacy; I know from experience that withdrawal actually
intensifies the pain. As an adult I finally recognized that I had
caused my own loneliness by expecting rejection, so I began to
compensate by deliberately reaching out to others.

But the old, remembered hurts came back manyfold when we moved and saw our friendly, outgoing daughter drawing into a shell as she began seventh grade in a large school among strangers. I watched her walking to and from school alone, her nose in a book. Reliving some of the pain of the past, I asked if she ate lunch alone. Yes. Were there ever others eating alone? Yes. How would she feel if one of them were to join her for lunch? Her face gave the obvious answer, and I assured her that others would feel the same way if she were to make the first move.

"It was awfully hard, and I didn't think I could do it," she remembers now, but she began reaching out. By the end of the school year she didn't want to miss a day and be away from her friends. In eighth grade someone commented, "You say hello to everyone, don't you?" In ninth grade she was elected vice-president of the school (the football hero was president), and chosen to represent her classmates on the student council the following year when they moved to a huge high school.

I was able to pass on to my daughter what I had learned about compensating, and she was helped before the problem became severe.

My niece was also helped through my daughter's experience. Beth is talented, willowy-slender—and tall. She had spent some lonely junior-high and high-school years, and beautiful Beth knew she was totally ugly. But she heard my daughter's story and determined to follow her example. Starting with her first day at college, Beth introduced herself as Tree (an old nickname) to everyone she met, knocked on the doors of her dorm to welcome newcomers, and looked for ways to be helpful. She enjoyed her new life on campus. Eventually, she was elected chairwoman of the Board of Women's Affairs, a high honor, and college was a delight to her. "And," says Tree, "nobody ever forgets my name!"

Both of these girls, like the writer of the letter to Abby, had learned to compensate for negative experiences.

An effective way to compensate for your feelings of

inadequacy is to help others feel more adequate. Eleanor Roosevelt was orphaned at ten, and her adolescence was apparently one of anguish. Homely and insecure, she never felt she belonged to anyone during her growing-up years. She is described by early contemporaries as a humorless introvert, unbelievably shy, unable to overcome personal insecurity, convinced of her own inadequacy. But she rose above it and became respected worldwide for her humanitarian work. It would seem from her life that one of the ways Mrs. Roosevelt helped herself was by helping others.

You can give yourself another handle on the art of compensation by disciplining yourself to develop a new skill. If you were totally free from the fear of failure, what would you like to do? Why not learn the basics and give it a try? It may take courage, but who knows? You might even enjoy it if

- you don't bite off too big of a chunk,
- you don't have unrealistic expectations,
- you're willing to learn by trial and error,
- you stay with it.

And with the enjoyment of using your new skill will come a new measure of self-confidence.

Still another way to compensate is by simply recognizing and appreciating what you *have* accomplished. Focus on those things you have learned to do well. Turn your mind deliberately on the positive in your life! You'll soon find it easier to see the positives in others, also—an added bonus.

Compensation is more than just a placebo; it can be an effective antidote for the ravages of supposed or real inadequacies on a person's fragile self-esteem.

CHANGE
Change is an even stronger antidote than compensation; it's the most effective self-esteem therapy available. But you can be open to change only when you realize you are on a par

with others, neither higher nor lower than they.

Satan has been called "the accuser of the brethren" in Revelation 12:10; he accuses you before God. But he also works overtime on *you*. He wants to keep you from having the healthy self-esteem God intends for you. Sometimes he fills you with feelings of superiority so you think it's others who need to change, not you. Other times he uses the criticism of family and friends to make you feel too inadequate to change.

God, though, wants to use those blows to your ego to conform you to the image of Christ. He can use the difficulties, the failures, the misunderstandings that come into your life to create in you Christlike qualities, including healthy self-esteem. Your part is to cooperate with him as he points out ways you need to change. (Change is dealt with more fully in the next chapter.)

Whether criticism is valid or not, when you react to it by laughing it off, becoming defensive, rationalizing, withdrawing into a shell, or striving mightily to conform, you are using only a placebo or a temporary anesthetic. Inside you, spilling over, there may be a turmoil of hurt, anger, frustration, bitterness, and—for that moment—the destruction of any vestige of healthy self-esteem.

If you desire the spiritual maturity and healthy self-esteem that God plans for you, choose to react differently when the next blow comes. Instead of using your customary coping reaction or deceiving yourself to dull the pain, go off in privacy and face the inner turmoil head-on. In a quiet place, ask God how he wants to use that pain, and what point of self-centeredness he wants you to abandon in exchange for one of his godly traits:

- your judgmental attitude for his love,
- your worry for his joy,
- your frustration for his peace,
- your irritation for his patience,
- your bitterness for his kindness,

- your selfishness for his goodness,
- your inconsistency for his faithfulness,
- your harshness for his gentleness,
- your quick temper for his self-control.

When you do this, the people of your world will see a clearer picture of God through your life. He will use your painful struggles to help you empathize with others who are hurting. You will become more like Christ and will better fulfill the purpose for which you were created: to glorify him.

So set aside your feeble attempts to cope with blows to your ego. Instead, let your Father use them to develop your character. Let God be God in you!

QUESTIONS FOR PERSONAL APPLICATION

1. Can you think of an instance in which you were inclined to criticize someone because you thought your priorities were better? Consider ways his life-style may have necessitated the priorities he chose. Consider why God may have chosen to give him his priorities and you yours. How might God be using him in ways you do not know? Consider that you cannot know all about another's life and therefore cannot make a judgment about his life-style.
2. What method of coping have you used most to counter blows to your self-esteem? Is it a healthy method? What would be better?
3. Are there wrong standards you have accepted because you have succumbed to peer or societal pressure?
4. It isn't what others say that hurts as much as what you tell yourself about what they've said. Thinking of what someone has recently said or done that has undermined your self-esteem, what could you tell yourself that could bring about growth and change in your life instead of a self-centered sense of inferiority?
5. How might you use compensation to build your own self-esteem? If you were totally free from the fear of failure, what would you like to do? Is it a possibility in your life? What could you do to implement this desire, following the guidelines on page 118?
6. Have you ever asked God to exchange one of his traits for one of yours? Which do you most desire to give up? Are you willing to be humbled so God can freely work in your life and bring about the needed change?

7. What valuable lessons have you learned—or can you learn—from painful experiences in your past? Consider creative avenues of service in which you might use these lessons positively.
8. How might you reach out from your own feelings of inadequacy to help others feel more adequate?
9. Consider some Bible verses that you could dwell on to arm yourself against future misunderstandings and criticism: Romans 5:3-8; 8:31-39; 12:14, 16, 21; 1 Corinthians 13; 15:57; 2 Corinthians 2:14; Philippians 1:6; 4:5-9, 11-13. Can you think of others?

QUESTIONS FOR GROUP DISCUSSION

1. Relate your experiences in sharing *anyhow* love this past week.
2. Consider the criticisms on page 107. What are some other digs or accusations people are prone to make? Write them down and discuss some possible extenuating circumstances others may not be aware of. Use your imagination—you might be shocked if you knew the valid reasons motivating some of the behavior you disagree with. Consider ways the person under attack might be obeying God. Commit yourself to avoiding judgments in the future, knowing you cannot truly "walk in another person's moccasins."
3. Rank the coping methods from 1 to 7 according to possible consequences, with 7 being the most positive.
4. Discuss your usual methods of coping with unhealthy self-esteem.
5. What should be your reaction to someone who is obviously displaying one of the negative coping patterns? Consider the patterns one by one. How might you build up the person whose hurt is disguised?
6. How can you make your children aware of coping patterns so they can choose the better ones and be sensitive to friends who are hiding their pain in other ways?
7. Discuss how much conformity is necessary and in what areas. What are some nonthreatening ways you can disccuss this issue with your families?
8. Share dreams of what you've always wanted to be able to do. Discuss how at least some of these dreams could become realities if you as a group were committed to encouraging and helping each other.
9. Discuss why we need to see ourselves as equals to each other in order to change.
10. Consider possible ways to reach out from your own feelings of inadequacy to help others feel more adequate.
11. Draw up a list of Bible verses with which you can arm yourselves against future blows to your self-esteem.

11   A Healing Balm
How to Draw on God's Strength

Perhaps all this talk about sibling rivalry and critical parents, put-downs and rejection, good looks and good grades has aroused bitter memories you'd rather forget. Have you ever wondered how to deal with hurtful experiences from your past?

You can't pretend they never happened, but at the same time you want to be free from the self-centered hang-ups they fostered. You may honestly want to let blows to your self-esteem make you more like Christ. But what can you do with hurts from the past that imprison you behind feelings of inadequacy?

Just as God provided his Son as the cure for the pride that plagues our daily lives, so he has prescribed a healing balm for deep wounds from the past that persistently reopen and fester. This balm can be applied to afflictions, to handicaps and disabilities, and any disappointments, loneliness, or bitterness you might experience. Some people may experience a once-for-all healing. Probably more will need to reapply the balm periodically when they find the pain returning.

The Apostle Paul had an affliction that troubled him. He

had been allowed to witness what no human had ever before seen or heard in order to prepare him for a special ministry. But then, to keep him from becoming puffed up, Paul was given "a thorn in the flesh, a messenger of Satan to buffet me" (2 Cor. 12:7, NASB), something to keep him dependent on God. It was apparently a humbling affliction, and continuously painful, and Paul asked God three times to remove it. God's answer? "My grace is sufficient for you, for my power is perfected in weakness" (2 Cor. 12:9, NASB).

Paul could have let his "thorn" fester; he could have become angry with God. He could have developed a complaining, self-centered attitude, hindering his ministry. But he didn't. Nor did he allow past blows and disadvantages to keep him looking inward. Driven out of town after town, distrusted and disliked by believers and nonbelievers, he didn't waste any time nursing a damaged ego. He got the message! He applied the balm:

Now I am glad to boast about how weak I am; I am glad to be a living demonstration of Christ's power, instead of showing off my own power and abilities. Since I know it is all for Christ's good, I am quite happy about "the thorn," and about insults and hardships, persecutions and difficulties; for when I am weak, then I am strong—the less I have, the more I depend on him. (2 Cor. 12:9-10, TLB)

The healing balm is God's strength—a strength that can replace all his children's weaknesses.

God makes no mistakes. Whether your weakness came at birth, or as the result of accident, illness, or unfair put-downs and disadvantages, he has allowed it into your life. He can use it. Perhaps to prick ballooning conceit. Perhaps to give you empathy. But always, so he can be reflected in your life. He will replace your weakness with his strength when, with steadfast mind, you place your trust in him (Isa. 26:3).

Certain attitudes, however, can prevent God's strength

from entering our lives. Are you, like Paul, content with weaknesses? Insults? Hardships? Persecutions? Difficulties? Or are you in the habit of complaining?

Are you clinging to hidden resentment and bitterness?

Are you angry about the opportunities you've missed?

You have a choice to make regarding your attitude toward painful circumstances. Will you let God use your circumstances for good? How you react to them—with anger or understanding, bitterness or forgiveness, hurtfulness or love—determines the extent to which God can replace your weakness with his strength.

ANGER—OR UNDERSTANDING?

In *Self-Talk*, Dr. David Stoop lays the cause of our anger before us. It's what we say and believe about what is happening (or what has happened) that causes us to be angry.

Since we make the choices about what we think, we are the ones who make the choice to be angry. . . . Whenever we become angry, we have initial feelings of hurt, frustration, or implied threat that we need to pay attention to. But when we get over those initial feelings, and still feel angry, it is because we are making demands on another person, or on a situation. . . .

The "shoulds," [including] must, gotta, ought to, and so forth . . . always reflect a demand that you are making on another person or on life and the world . . . a demand that we cannot effectively guarantee will be met. And that's the source of our anger. . . . The key to defusing your anger is to identify these demands and change them into wants and desires.[1]

We may not actually state, "He shouldn't have done that to me," but that's what we really mean. Stoop suggests we make a chart listing what makes us angry in one column, the "shoulds" or demands we have attached to that person or situation (thoughts that *create* anger) in the second column, and those demands restated in the form of wants, wishes, or desires (thoughts that *control* anger) in the third column. Every time you begin to feel angry about the situation, take out the sheet and read over the third column several times.[2]

Triggers Anger	Shoulds/Musts or Demands	Restated as Wants
My son loses his textbook.	He should know better.	I wish he were more responsible.
	He should have taken care of it sooner.	One of these days he will understand that he only hurts himself.
	He should be more responsible.	
	I shouldn't have to tell him.	I sure will be glad when he takes care of these things without my help.

BITTERNESS—OR FORGIVENESS?

God cannot replace our weaknesses with his strengths while we are harboring grudges and blaming others for our inadequacies. He can't bring healing until we correct our thinking about those who have insulted us and in other ways brought difficulties into our lives. He can't bring healing until we are willing to forgive.

Forgiving someone doesn't mean you condone sin. Christ is our example. We hurt him with our willfulness, our overactive concern with self, our shabby treatment of others, and our habit of ignoring him. He does not approve of our sins, yet he wants to forgive them. He cared enough to pay the price for them with his life. That's forgiveness in action, and all we have to do to receive it is to ask God to apply Christ's death to our lives.

If you then follow God's example by deciding to forgive those who have hurt you, you too will pay a price. You won't be able to retaliate, shun, accuse, or condemn those who have caused you pain. They may go scot-free, unchanged, and, therefore, able to hurt you again.

In some circumstances, such as when physical harm has occurred, Christians may find it necessary to confront, accuse, and even testify against someone. But even then, the attitude of the heart needs to be one of forgiveness. If you choose *not* to forgive, you still have to pay a price—the price of bitterness, one of the curses of self-centeredness.

Bitterness is such a potent paralysis of mind, soul and spirit that it can freeze our reason, emotions and all our responses. . . . Both love and hate can soon sour to apathy, indifference and cold neutrality. Bitterness cuts the nerve to our emotions. They go dead—like paralysis.[3]

How much better to pay the price of forgiveness than the price of bitterness!

Forgiveness is a free gift of love or it is nothing of value. . . . If you hold back forgiveness until the offender deserves *it, forget it! That's not forgiveness! Forgive immediately! Forgive when the first hurt is felt! Quickly. Unhesitatingly. Immediately! Knowing the great value of time [we] cannot afford to let it slip by in futile pain. . . . The man who follows Christ . . . hurries to forgive.*

There is no forgiveness without genuine acceptance of the other person as he is. . . . The greatest test of continual forgiveness is the daily kind of forgiving love which gives and takes, freely accepting the bruises and hurts of loving. No matter how difficult the blows life deals us.[4]

If life had dealt you no blows, perhaps you would sense no need for God's strength. You could manage very well without him, and others would see *you,* not Christ. Paul is right: The less we have, the more we depend on God. Be grateful for your weaknesses!

HURTFULNESS—OR LOVE?

Unfortunately, your lifetime struggle with pride doesn't produce only anger and bitterness within you. It also gives you the capacity to hurt others. How many times have you caused others hurt by

- snubbing,
- being sarcastic,
- criticizing,
- showing disdain,
- communicating disinterest?

These actions, too, can stifle the power of God in your life.

Sometimes our hurtful ways are so subtle we don't even recognize what we're doing:

I had been a Christian for many years before my eyes were opened to see the superior attitude that had been so much a part of my life. Not that I was guilty of so many verbal put-downs; a Christian doesn't do that, and besides, I didn't like it when others criticized me. No, it was a condescension, the inner opinion that my ways were better. It was an inability to really love people and see them as equal.

What are some practical steps we can take to change the way we treat others, as well as change our attitude toward the way they treat us?

An important first step is to examine our thoughts regarding our relationships and circumstances, from childhood and the present. In their book *Telling Yourself the Truth,* Backus and Chapian observe that our feelings are caused by *what we tell ourselves* about our circumstances, whether in words or in attitudes. We can tell ourselves either truths or lies. We need to locate the misbeliefs in our thoughts, remove them, and replace them with the truth.[5]

Remember the woman whose twin sister died when they were small? She related:

I overheard a relative say, "Isn't it a shame the pretty one died?" I grew up feeling guilty, knowing I must be a disappointment to my parents, and that I could never measure up.

For many years this woman had lied to herself: "I'm not as pretty as my twin was. I should have been the one to die; she should have lived. I'm not as valuable as she was; my parents can never be satisfied with me." Now middle-aged, she is finally able to recognize the truth: "Beauty doesn't determine my value, and God has a plan for my life!"

If your mother-in-law—or someone close to you—is critical of you, it's easy to tell yourself lies. "I can't ever be good enough for her. Something must be wrong with me." Or, "She's a hateful woman; I don't care what she thinks." The result? Defensiveness, anger, and fragile self-esteem. When you're around your mother-in-law or friend, you are tense, cold, and unloving, drawing even more criticism from her. The truth? There are several possibilities:

- Perhaps she has a point; maybe you *could* improve in some area she has been criticizing.
- Perhaps, if she's your mother-in-law, she has found it hard to give up her son to another woman because of her own deep needs; perhaps, if she's your friend, she finds it hard to share you with other people.
- Perhaps many painful experiences have fostered an unhealthy self-esteem and a critical spirit within her.

Whatever the truth is—perhaps all of the above—your relative or friend needs affirmation from you—approval, encouragement, affection, and warmth. You must tell yourself that her attitude toward you does not in any way lessen your value. God has already established your worth, and people do not nullify what he has done!

What are your misbeliefs? Can you locate the lies? "I'm ugly." "People don't like me." "I do dumb things." "I always sound stupid." "I'm not as valuable as those who are prettier and more capable and more intelligent and better educated."

Holding onto misbeliefs can hurt not only you but also those around you.

Once you locate your misbeliefs, set about replacing them with the truth. "These things don't determine my value. It simply isn't true to say I'm not as important or as good as others. I have many good qualities. God has given me talents to use; he loves me and he values me."

What you think and believe determines how you feel and act. That's why it is important to recognize the lies that fill your thoughts. They can create anger, pain, resentment, self-pity, and self-doubt. The truth, in contrast, will fill you with love, peace, patience, hope, and confidence.

God wants you to draw on his strength to overcome your weaknesses. He is committed to using the thorns in your life, no matter how painful some of them may be, to prepare you to be his special compassionate servant. He says, "For I know the plans that I have for you . . . plans for welfare and not for calamity to give you a future and a hope" (Jer. 29:11, NASB). You can choose to focus your thoughts on him and his good plans for you.

Be grateful for the problems: His strength is infinitely better than your own! Let that reassurance be soothing balm to your troubled life.

QUESTIONS FOR PERSONAL APPLICATION

1. Write down one "thorn" in your life. Then list all of the possible ways God could use it for good.
2. List the weaknesses that are in your life because of past hurts, insults, hardships, abuses. In what ways are you bitter or angry about them? Who do you blame for them?
3. What possible inner needs may have provoked people to make attacks on you? Will you forgive them?
4. What is the difference between "excusing" and "forgiving"?
5. List two ways in which a family member makes you angry. Put them on the chart suggested by Dr. Stoop (page 126).
6. Is there someone you may be hurting through an attitude of condescension or even open criticism? How will you change your attitude?

7. Has this chapter led you to identify some key misbeliefs in your life? Can you also recognize the truths with which you need to replace them?
8. What truth might you learn about yourself from past criticisms? What truth might you become aware of concerning the criticizer?
9. Have you come to the point where you can say "Thank you, God" for your weaknesses? When you are aware of specific ones again, seek his strength to replace them.
10. At what time each day will you specifically thank God for his goodness to you and his high estimation of you?

QUESTIONS FOR GROUP DISCUSSION

1. How would you explain to someone Paul's words, "For when I am weak, then I am strong" (2 Cor. 12:10, NASB)? What are some of the ways we prevent God from replacing our weaknesses with his strength?
2. List some typical "should" statements that we make in anger. In what way do they reflect a demand we are making? Restate these "shoulds" as "wants." (See pages 125-126.)
3. Discuss question 4 from Questions for Personal Application.
4. If we forgive someone, in what ways do we pay the price of the hurt we are forgiving? What price do we pay when we choose not to forgive? In what way is the latter price worse to pay?
5. What are some inner needs that may have provoked unkindnesses, even personal attacks, directed against you? Can you forgive the attacker?
6. How can we change our thoughts when hurts pop into our minds again?
7. How does a condescending attitude manifest itself? Can it be hidden?
8. Do you feel free to discuss any newly recognized misbeliefs with the group? What are the truths with which you will replace them?
9. Give some examples of how what you think and believe determines how you feel and act. Then cite possible changes in those thought patterns and the corresponding effects on behavior.

12   RX: A Sense of Belonging
Where Do You Fit In?

To be emotionally healthy, we need to feel that we belong, that we have worth, and that we are competent. Each of these needs is equally important.

Norman Wakefield sees the three needs as interlocking circles:[1]

SELF-ESTEEM

Waylon Ward has suggested the image of a three-legged milking stool to illustrate them.[2] A person's self-esteem will be in a precarious position if one or more of the legs is too short:

SELF-ESTEEM

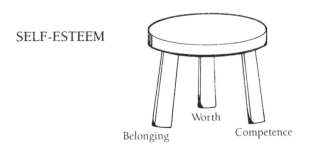

Worth

Belonging   Competence

We've chosen to use a circle that has three equal segments to illustrate the basic parts of self-esteem. The first of the three segments is *belonging.*

SELF-ESTEEM

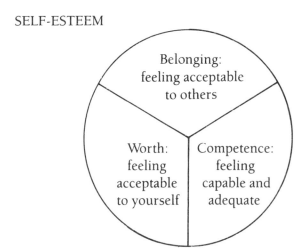

Belonging:
feeling acceptable
to others

Worth:
feeling
acceptable
to yourself

Competence:
feeling
capable and
adequate

Belonging: Having a sense of security and identity with others who love, accept, and support me.[3]

"Where do I fit in?" is a question asked by many people, old and young alike.

Four-year-old Billie was a strawberry blonde, curly-haired charmer who didn't know where she belonged or to whom. Neither she nor her many babysitters ever knew when her mom would return for her—tonight, tomorrow, or next week.

Billie would lock her arms around the neck of any unwary woman who stooped to talk to her. This left two options: pry her arms open or pick her up. If picked up, Billie would ask, with shining eyes, "Will you be my mommy?" When she was with us, every man who rang our doorbell was greeted with the cry, "Daddy!"—startling salesmen and betraying her mother's life-style.

A few days after she was placed with our family, I had an evening meeting to attend, and Billie and my husband chauffeured me. But as Jim dressed Billie in hat, coat, mittens, and boots on that cold January evening, she seemed increasingly uneasy. "Do you wike me?" she asked softly. "Are you mad to me?" And then, "Can I come back here?" This was the heart of her unease, we came to understand.

When Jim dropped me off at my meeting, Billie became hysterical, demanding that they return for me immediately, and Jim had a difficult two hours before she finally fell into exhausted sleep. Early the next morning I wakened to find those blue eyes almost touching my nose as Billie bent over me. When she saw my eyes open she said in a whisper, "You did come back!" Later, in a rare quiet moment, she asked wistfully, "Mommy, will you be my real mommy?"

In the six months Billie lived with us before returning to her mother, we never left the house without her standing at the door asking anxiously, "Are you coming back?" We never took her anywhere without hearing that uneasy question, "Can I come back here?" And she never stopped greeting perfect strangers with, "Daddy!" or, "Will you be my mommy?"

Billie didn't feel she belonged anywhere, and her insecurity was deep-rooted and intense. An inadequate sense of belonging isn't always as emotionally damaging as it was in Billie's life, but it always causes some harm and it always hurts.

Not to belong is to be shut out. It means being excluded from the group at school or at church or even at home. It's moving and finding the new neighbors cold, new coworkers nonaccepting, new classmates cliquish. It's being deserted or divorced or widowed. But most of all, it's not having the support and strength of a family.

The lack of family love in eighteen-year-old Tricia's life resulted in sad, extreme behavior.

The youngest of five children, Tricia had known from early childhood that she was unplanned, an unwelcome intrusion into the family. She was the one who had ruined Mother's figure. On a regular basis during her teenage years, Tricia slit her wrists and overdosed on sleeping pills and tranquilizers.

Lacking any sense of family security, Tricia reached desperately for attention and affirmation. After she had lived with us for a month we told her that another girl, who was seventeen and pregnant, would be joining the family soon. Tricia spent a very quiet, pensive day, and in the evening she finally opened up: "Right now Jim and Holli and Laurie and I each have 25 percent of you. When Megan comes, we'll have only 20 percent."

Even casual visitors were a threat to Tricia, competition for my time and attention and affection. The time I spent reading the newspaper angered her.

Two years and several other placements later, bubbly sixteen-year-old Carole came for a weekend trial visit. Afterwards, Tricia said, "You want to know how I feel about Carole moving in, so I'll tell you how I feel. I don't get enough attention around here as it is, and with her here I'll get even less!"

For Tricia and Billie and many others, a lack of belonging has caused pain and emotional damage that isn't easily healed.

Belonging creates strength and security. Belonging is being wanted and loved for who you are, warts and all. Even if you don't always feel loved and accepted by your family, you can derive some comfort from knowing you're included in the clan. Having a place within the same group of people day after day and year after year—a family of some kind, even a group of friends—is crucial to self-esteem.

What's the magic formula that can assure a child he belongs? Some important ingredients include:

- feeling accepted by other family members,
- receiving loving discipline,
- enjoying time together,
- having a strong family identity,
- basking in a warm atmosphere.

ACCEPTANCE

Someone has estimated that one out of four Americans is lonely—and teenagers make up the loneliest group of all. Young people who may join a close-knit group such as a cult are desperately hungry for love, approval, and guidance. The cult gives them a strong sense of belonging and a form of acceptance they didn't find outside. Cults capitalize on the deep need of every human being to be wanted, and unhappy, rootless young people are particularly vulnerable.

Why are so many young people rootless? Because nobody cares enough. Nobody accepts them in spite of their failing. They've known acceptance in the past only because of their successes, and that's not enough. When home doesn't provide for the basic emotional need of belonging, Satan will provide a substitute family. That is the genesis of gangs and cults.

Being accepted and loved the way you are provides a warm blanket of security. A supportive climate frees you to explore and make mistakes without being judged. But when what you do or don't do serves as the basis for acceptance, feelings of belonging are destroyed.

Andrea's mother had never allowed her to help with the housework because Andrea didn't do anything to her mom's satisfaction. Mother said she could work faster by herself, without interference. Andrea had grown up with criticism, harshness, and anger directed at her when she made mistakes. Emotionally deprived, she believed the first boy who said he loved her, and she married him—when she was sixteen and pregnant. But Jack was too young, at seventeen, to handle the burden of being a husband and a father, and he continued the downgrading Andrea had known all her life; she couldn't please him, either.

When Andrea moved next door to us with her husband and two small sons, she "knew" herself to be ugly and worthless. She was unusually attractive and a good worker who was appreciated by her boss. But that wasn't enough to compensate for the negative input she had received all her life. She "knew" herself to be totally inadequate as a wife, a mother, a cook, a housekeeper—as a person.

Andrea committed her life to Christ soon after we met. But for three years, in spite of her eager Bible study and dedicated prayer life, she experienced little growth, no real joy, and no assurance in her Christian walk. She was totally bound up in the "I'm-such-a-terrible-person" syndrome. "How can God love me?" she often asked me.

Then her marriage disintegrated, more proof of her inadequacies. Andrea and the little boys moved in with us temporarily, and one day when I returned home she met me at the door, very upset: "Mom, you're going to hate me! I broke your casserole cover!" I assured her that a piece of aluminum foil would work fine until we could find a replacement—no big deal. Several days later, when I was putting foil paper on the same dish, Andrea blurted, "Oh, I know you must hate me!" "Yes, I sure do hate you, honey," I laughed, giving her a hug.

Soon afterward she and the boys moved into their own apartment, but not before we had begun to notice a change in Andrea. Her long hair, which usually fell into her face, framing an unhappy, sullen expression, was now brushed back. Andrea was smiling a lot and beginning to evidence healthy spiritual growth and understanding. A more positive attitude was replacing her negative mind-set.

Andrea blossomed; her walk with Christ grew stronger. One day I told her that everyone was talking about the change in her. She was well aware of the change and seemed surprised that I didn't realize how and when it began. "Remember when I broke your casserole cover? I expected you to kick the boys and me out of the house that night. I really thought you would hate me for it. But instead, it didn't even matter to you; it didn't seem to make any difference. You treated me the same as before. You still loved me in the same way. And it finally dawned on me what you've been trying to tell me all this time—it finally got through my thick skull! If you can love me in spite of the things I've done and the way I am, then I guess God can, too!"

A broken casserole cover was so inconsequential to me. But God used the incident to give Andrea a clearer picture of what he is like. What it means to be accepted in Christ. What it means to belong.

Molly heard the story of the prodigal son, and her reaction was a delighted one: "Man, that's really cool! I mean, your own folks kick you out and call the cops on you. But God—wow, that's really neat—he just wants you to come back!" How many people need to know just that? Many imagine rejection everywhere, even from God, because of nonacceptance at home.

Yet God assures us repeatedly that he loves us and accepts us without reservation. "While we were yet sinners, Christ died for us" (Rom. 5:8, NASB). We don't have to measure up in order to be loved by him. He originated the supportive climate! He accepts us as we are. And he will help us love and accept others as they are.

COMMUNICATION
Our baby-sitter was totally frustrated by our two-year-old's repeated complaint: "I dots a yore on my weets!" She finally

appealed to me, and I translated: Holli had a sliver in her big toe, a sore on her feet.

Good communication is another obvious aspect of belonging, but it can be elusive—and sometimes, like a "good cold," a contradiction in terms. We hear, for example, of the wife who says to her husband when he's trying to fall asleep, "Let me know when you're too sleepy to argue; I have something to tell you."

Of course, good communication requires careful listening. It's obvious—but so difficult. Listening takes work and effort.

I grew up reading, hearing my mother's voice call, and intending to respond "at the end of this sentence . . . at the end of this paragraph . . . at the end of this chapter."

When my husband went overseas in World War II, I spent a lot of time out on the farm with his parents. There I learned to stop reading immediately and answer even the most casual comments because being ignored was not accepted. I made my new mother-in-law angry a few times, and it was a good lesson for me. But I am still guilty of continuing to work at a task while conversing.

One teenager we know demands in exasperation almost daily, "Mother, look at me so you can hear me!" Listening involves eye contact, because nonverbal messages carry more weight than words. One source suggests that a message has three components:

- actual words or content make up 7 percent of the message;
- tone of voice constitutes another 38 percent;
- nonverbal language accounts for 55 percent.[4]

In other words, if you continue to read the paper, peel potatoes, or pound a nail while someone is talking to you, you will miss out on the message he is communicating through gestures, posture, and facial expression. If actual words make up less than 10 percent of the message, with body language saying even more than the tone of voice, then eye contact is essential for good communication.

Gloria learned how easy it is to miss the silent message:

My twelve-year-old seemed so satisfied with herself that I found it irritating. I felt I must convince her that she needed to improve herself. After all, it's my duty as a mother to make her aware of her deficiencies so she can do something about them. So all winter I've been saying things like, "Sara, if you'd wash your face more often you wouldn't have so many pimples." But I just felt ignored and frustrated. Then this spring I came across a piece of paper in Sara's handwriting:

	Sept. 8	What to do	Later
skin	yuk	wash oftener	
figure	too fat	diet	
hair	awful	brush every night	
hands	ugly	use hand cream	
nails	horrible	stop biting	

The last column was blank; apparently Sara never saw any improvement. I was heartsick. All this time I should have been building her up, encouraging her good points, and praising her efforts. I just had no idea she felt that way about herself!

How can we hear what our children are feeling? We can start when they are very small as we listen to their earnest absurdities with open ears, without laughing or mocking. If you take the time today to listen to your child's account of all nine innings of the ball game, or even to hear his replay of the whole movie, tomorrow you might hear him share something very personal, something of his deep feelings or needs. Confidences are hard to share unless you know you will be heard and accepted. Unless conversation is the norm when children are small, it won't happen spontaneously when they become teenagers. If you don't receive much response to your questions today, maybe it's because you didn't listen to yesterday's answers.

Our daughter wrote from college on her dad's birthday with a long list of things she appreciated about him, including, "You always kept the dinner conversation lively." And she certainly didn't mean he did all the talking! He asked questions, he listened, and he drew out discussion, both thoughtful and fun. He often had a joke or two to tell, and he laughed at all of his children's jokes. No matter what happened during his day, at dinnertime his interest in his family superseded everything else.

Dinnertime is ideal for family conversation. Here you can learn how your children view life. Make sure to recognize each person at the table and show that you consider the events of his or her day important. Teach your children to look for incidents to share and topics to discuss. Talk about school, about friends, about God. Try encouraging discussion by throwing out some premise your children won't agree with (perhaps you won't either), and letting them try to argue you out of your position. Keep real conflict from the dinner table, though! A prickly subject can often be best discussed during a brisk walk—after you each have agreed to disagree.

By your own example, you will encourage your children to listen to other people. We all need people who talk *with* us, not *at* us. Do you care enough to try to walk in another person's shoes, even if what he is saying is entirely outside of your experience? Your children will learn to listen with that kind of awareness and concern if you model it for them.

The consequences of poor communication in the home are somber. When nonverbal messages aren't understood, or you can't express opinions without being rebuked or laughed at, you learn not to say anything. You may build up a wall, shutting others out.

Fortunately, that's a learned behavior—and it's never too

late to change it. You can, by a deliberate act of your will, begin to communicate again with other people. When you recognize that you have withdrawn because your opinion wasn't respected when you were growing up, or isn't valued now by someone who is important in your life, you can determine to make a change.

You cheat yourself when you shut off communication with friends, parents, or children—and you cheat them, too. You can choose to limit those relationships, but in doing so you harm your self-esteem and theirs.

You also cheat yourself when you limit communication with God. He urges us to come boldly to him in prayer. Because of Christ's death and resurrection, we now have free access to the Father. Do you limit your conversation with him because you don't understand his nature? He bends his ear, longing to hear your voice or the softest cry of your heart.

Stevie told Santa he'd like a box of crayons. Santa, who had been hearing requests all day for bikes, wagons, and dolls, urged Stevie on: "Oh, come on now, you want more than crayons!" "Some pencils," said Stevie, and he slid off Santa's lap.

"You do not have because you do not ask" (James 4:2, Amp). Like Stevie, sometimes we ask for so little. If you don't understand the power of God in your life, you'll be satisfied with crayons and pencils. But he offers you his wisdom, his attitudes, and his attributes. You have *all* of him when you have Christ.

Whether it's poor communication or another weakness you face, he knows your needs. And he listens.

LOVING DISCIPLINE

How does discipline contribute to a sense of belonging? Sally, fifteen, wrote to her foster parents, "You are the only people in my whole life who really cared enough to make me go by the rules." It is impossible to feel secure without rules to go by. Fences. Training.

Discipline—preventive and corrective, with the scales heavily weighted on the preventive side—is basically marking out the boundaries and enforcing them consistently. Anyone who misses this important ingredient during his growing-up years may still suffer the effects in adulthood: insecurity, uneasiness, a sense of "Where do I belong, and who really cares?"

A child who is undisciplined may have a subtle fear of not belonging to the clan. He senses instinctively that "if they really loved me, they wouldn't let me act this way." Of course, he will never admit that he craves the security of fences, and he'll cover up his insecurity with a facade of indifference, hostility, or rebellion.

Peggy, for example, regularly flouted authority. Yet one night she confided to her surprised foster parents that she felt sorry for a friend because "her mother doesn't care what time she gets home."

The authority figures in Peggy's life had been harsh and abusive, and she was an angry child. When she came to us at the age of thirteen she hated the world in general and all authority in particular. She had no concept of love except in romantic terms; when I put my arm around her shoulders she shrugged me off and demanded, "What are you, a homo?"

I asked Peggy one day how her Sunday school class had gone and she simpered mockingly, "Oh, God loves you; he'll forgive you anything." And then she exploded: "It makes me sick! He wants you to be his slave! Do what he says and he'll reward you like a dog." She switched briefly to a mocking voice: " 'Love me, believe in my Son, and I'll give you eternal life.' Well, big deal! Who wants it?" If God was real, which she doubted, she hated him.

We didn't expect Peggy to finish eighth grade. She was into

*drugs and freaked out on LSD her first Christmas with us.
Someone in her circle of friends was always running away.
She clung to kindred spirits, other rebellious adolescents who
shared a sense of rejection by their families.*

*For some reason, Peggy never ran away, but she did try to
prove to herself and to us that she didn't have to follow our
rules. The drug use dropped significantly after two years, but
the deliberate disobedience didn't. Many times we almost gave
up on her. Yet from time to time we saw a softening, little hints
of affection to encourage us and keep us going. And sometimes
she would open up and talk about her many fears and her
experiences at home—the hard things.*

*When she was seventeen and in her last year of high school,
Peggy said about a friend of hers, "Do you know what Amy's
problem is? Her mother always let her do anything she
wanted!" I fought down the laugh that bubbled up in me; I had
been hearing for four years that Peggy wasn't going to tell
her children what to do and how to live. So I said very care-
fully, "But Peggy, isn't that the kind of parent you always
wanted?"*

*Peggy hesitated a moment, and then I was rewarded with a
small, rueful grin. "Well, I used to think you just wanted to
boss me around and run my life. Now I know it's because you
really care!"*

*Not long after that, Peggy prayed, "Well, God, you've been
chasing me for a long time, and I guess it's time for me to quit
running." And she asked Christ to come into her life.*

What happened to Peggy? With more or less firm, reason-
able rules, she gradually began to feel that someone cared.
Slowly, ever so slowly, she began to feel secure and loved.
It's no mystery. God explains it clearly: "He who loves [his
child] is careful to discipline him" (Prov. 13:24, NIV).

God our heavenly Father provides the absolutes and the
guidelines, as well as the chastening that we need to feel
secure. We can follow his example in our homes.

TIME

"You are important to me" is the message we convey when we share time with others. Do you need to budget time for others? Giving someone your undivided attention even for a few minutes of talking, listening, playing, or walking is worth many hours of just being in the house together. Even sharing work creatively or occasionally enjoying a TV program together can accomplish the same goal.

Waylon Ward suggests that self-image basically hinges on three questions: How do I look? How do I do (in comparison with others)? How important am I? And the answer to the third, says Ward, begins with the amount of time a parent gives his child. Time becomes a grading stick for the child's importance. Do you allot more time for TV, sports, hobbies, church activities, or PTA than for your family? The message gets through. Ward says his three-year-old daughter once asked, "Mommy, do you love me as much as you do your flowers?"[5]

Also crucial is the quality of your time together. Do you enjoy your child? Do you enjoy the time you spend with him? Your enjoyment of him helps him feel good about himself. Some studies indicate that American fathers, who may think they spend a lot of time with their children, average *less than five minutes per week* of interaction with them. What a tragedy! What's the answer? Careful attention to planned quality time.

One thoughtful father who has two small sons sets aside one evening a week for dinner with individual members of his family. (McDonalds is the usual choice.) The first week of the month is reserved for son number one, the second for son number two, the third for his wife, and the fourth for the whole family. Another busy father with adolescent daughters takes each one out on an inexpensive dinner date once a month. (He doesn't forget their mother, either.)

Time alone with each child is so important—time for talking and working together, time for getting to know each other, time for learning what a child thinks and how he looks at the world.

Equally important is time spent together as a family for fun activities. You might try games that aren't highly competitive, as well as those that teach how to be a gracious winner or a graceful loser. For an activity that builds skills, choose from skating, swimming, bowling, fishing, gymnastics, biking, and hiking. Or for leisure, take a casual walk, identifying trees, weeds, insects, or constellations.

Most important of all are times centered around God at home and at church with other members of his family. He won't force his way into your family circle, but he waits to be included. He created you for fellowship with him, and his presence can make your family devotions the ultimate quality time!

FAMILY IDENTITY

When teenagers were asked in a survey, "What is your greatest fear?" the most frequent answer was not nuclear war, as one might expect. It was "the loss of my family." The family is a source of belonging, even during the normal trauma and friction of a child's adolescent years.

"I'm happy to be a part of this family" is an attitude that creates a sense of belonging. It begins with the parents and spreads to each member of the family. *Happy the family whose members enjoy each other!*

All family members should be encouraged to

- speak well of each other,
- indicate pride in each other,
- give and receive honest compliments.

Giving sincere compliments, freely and without embarrassment, should be a top priority for every Christian—a habit pattern! It's an especially important habit within the family, where it needs to be taught.

Norman Wakefield, in his multimedia presentation on family self-esteem, suggests other ways to build a strong family identity, and with it, feelings of belonging.

1. *Plan a day a month during which one family member is honored with a special meal of his choice, and family members express appreciation for him through art, music, or other creative means.*

2. *As part of table conversation, have each family member share what he did that day that he feels good about.*

3. *Design a family shield or coat of arms, especially if your family name is different enough to elicit teasing from schoolmates. It may include a family verse, a symbol of the family's greatest strength, three words that describe the family, or a symbol of each family member.*

4. *Choose one family member. Have other family members share or write one thing they appreciate about that person. Repeat the process for the second family member until each person has had an opportunity to be praised.*

5. *Send letters to each other to express appreciation. Parental example teaches children to speak well of others!*

6. *Brainstorm things for which to compliment people; compile a chart. Whenever a family member receives a compliment, he can write the complimenter's name on the chart.*[6]

Another possibility is to draw names for a secret pal in your family, and do special things for him or her for one week.

Family customs and ethnic traditions encourage a sense of family identity, and grandparents and other relatives can play a part in demonstrating those traditions.

But perhaps the most crucial way to strengthen individual and family life is to cultivate relationships within the church that provide continuing day-to-day interaction with people who care.

As a part of building family identity, do not hesitate to say, "We don't do that in this family!" when confronting wrong behavior. We parents should make it a point to instill that thought in the young minds of our children. Children like to be proud of their parents. We can increase their respect by standing up for beliefs in a gentle but firm way as we are advised in 1 Peter 3:15. Children need to be reassured that it's all right to be different. They, too, can take pride in those values that make their family "unique."

A WARM ATMOSPHERE

What can replace a warm, inviting home? Everyone enjoys returning to a place where they feel welcome.

Parents might be pleasantly surprised to know that teenagers consider home to be a *refuge* from their peer group—the very peer group that encourages antagonism between them and their teenager!

Friends need to feel welcome, also, even though they may bring noise and confusion with them. You'll sometimes long for peace and privacy. Just remember, you'll have more than you want all too soon; the nest empties suddenly.

A young boy living at home again after a while in a foster home wrote the following letter to his caseworker:

Dear Miss Johnson,
Here are 19 reasons why I want to go back to the Smiths:
  1. They have good food there and plenty of it.
  2. There's plenty of clothes to wear.
  3. There is laughter there.
  4. The roof doesn't leak.
  5. It's quiet there and I can study.
  6. They have lots of visitors.
  7. It's close to sports.
  8. They have a car and they take us places.
  9. We have a bike there and things to do.
 10. They give us an allowance.
 11. They have real beds and I can sleep good.
 12. They don't get mad about nothing.
 13. Their TV works.

14. They teach me good.
15. They remember birthdays and Christmas.
That's only 15 reasons, but there really are 19!
Your friend,
Tommy

Much of Tommy's list reflects the essence of belonging. A sense of being wanted and respected, a supportive climate, quality family times—all add up to a comfortable, warm atmosphere, an inviting home in which to be growing up.

THE BEST WAY TO BELONG

I was the third of six children, and I was the sickly one. My parents often showed me special attention and concern for that reason. Although it was never said, I always felt I was their favorite. Mother was very affectionate, and she let me know I was special to them. She repeated privately to me anything positive Daddy said to her about me. Inwardly, I felt sorry for my siblings because they didn't have that special place, but I never mentioned it to anyone.

When we were all grown and scattered around the country, we began a round-robin letter, and one day I was surprised to read in my kid brother's letter: ". . . being the folks' favorite, as the baby of the family. . . ." I smiled to myself and opened my older sister's letter. She began by addressing herself to the youngest: ". . . I was interested to read that you considered yourself the folks' favorite child; I always thought I was! Mother used to say she didn't know how she could get along without me, and I figured she couldn't!"

So who was the favorite? No one. We were six children fortunate enough to grow up with anyhow love—a special kind of parenting. We knew how highly we were regarded by our parents, and we didn't want to hurt or disappoint them. Belonging? We had it!

But what if you didn't have this experience in your home? What if you grew up devoid of a sense of belonging?

There is no way to go back and change the past. Does that mean you are hopelessly locked into an emotional lack? Is there no way out?

Of course, there is. Healing is available. God offers each of us a clear sense of belonging—and all that we need to develop it:

- total acceptance and security,
- communication through his Word and prayer,
- definitive guidelines,
- companionship with other believers,
- a strong identity within his family,
- a heavenly home.

God wants so much for us to belong! He has adopted us into his family, and he offers us everything we need to feel at home there. We are his heirs, along with all our brothers and sisters in Christ. Together we are the body of Christ, the family of God, strugglers helping each other grow, children needing parenting and family ties.

The family of God is a source of parenting that can supplement our own imperfect upbringing.

There is no question but that your parents failed you as parents. All parents fail their children, and yours are no exception. No parent is ever adequate for the job of being a parent, and there is no way not to fail at it. No parent ever has enough love or wisdom or maturity. . . . No parent ever succeeds.

This means that part of your task . . . is to supplement what your parents have given you, to find other sources of parenting. You need more mothering than your mother could give you, more fathering than your father had to offer, more brothering and sistering than you got from your siblings.[7]

The family of God can help meet your need for oneness with others, your hunger for belonging.

Because of his kindness you have been saved through trusting Christ. . . . Now you are no longer strangers to God and foreigners to heaven, but you are members of God's very own family, citizens of God's country, and you belong in God's household with every other Christian. (Eph. 2:8a, 19, TLB)

You belong! You have a place! You are needed! You fit into the picture, and it isn't complete without you.

QUESTIONS FOR PERSONAL APPLICATION

1. List the groups to which you positionally belong (immediate family, extended family, work force, church, and so forth). Star the ones in which you feel truly accepted. List the persons or groups among whom you would like to be accepted but feel you are not. What do you see as the barriers?
2. List persons you know who may not feel accepted in your groups. What steps could you take to help them feel closer to the rest of you?
3. Is there someone you need to accept as he is?
4. Have you limited or shut off communication with friends, parents, or children? In what ways has this behavior cheated you and them? How can you begin to change it?
5. How do you rate as a listener? Could you improve? Will you begin to really listen to the others in your circle?
6. What gift of time will you give to those who need to know they are important to you? Make a date with your mate. Go for a walk or for a cup of coffee or dinner and communicate. Why would a monthly date with each of your children be important? In what ways might it build better relationships between you and them?
7. Do you take part in activities at your church? What have you done to reach out and help others feel a sense of belonging there? What could you do?
8. Of Norman Wakefield's six suggestions for improving family identity, communication, and quality time (page 148), which two would work best in your family?

QUESTIONS FOR GROUP DISCUSSION

1. Brainstorm ways we build belonging, worth, and competence in our children. Also think of ways we tear down these important dimensions of self-esteem.
2. In what ways does knowing that you belong to a group build self-esteem?
3. When have you experienced a lack of belonging?

4. Which of the six listed ingredients of belonging do you think is most important? Why?
5. In what ways might a monthly date with each child build better relationships in the home?
6. Discuss some activities available in your community that would be good for family times together. What special things can you do with each child individually? With your mate?
7. How can we encourage our children to take pride in values that make their families unique?
8. When would teenagers consider home to be a refuge from their peer group? What could you as parents further do to provide that refuge?
9. Does viewing the family of God as another source of parenting and belonging influence your involvement with church activities? What could you do individually and as a class to encourage a sense of belonging among people there?
10. What in the gospel can help give a person a sense of belonging?

13   RX: A Sense of Worth
How Important Are You?

Worth: Being affirmed as a person of value; being cherished and respected.[1]

After Lois attempted suicide, she was advised by her counselors to concentrate on what she did well, using compensation to cope with her feelings of worthlessness. By following their recommendations, she has been able to lead a productive life. But now she wants to go beyond achievement—she wants to feel that she is a person of worth just for herself.

The same is true for Marie. Because she is talented, she is continually affirmed for her abilities. But she says, "I need to know I'm valuable for just being *me*, not because of what I'm able to produce."

Lois and Marie express an identical need; they are asking for an affirmation of their worth.

To believe in your own worth means you think you're

OK—you count. But often we are our own worst enemies.

- Do you imagine slights where none were intended?
- Do you put yourself down in your thoughts and conversation?
- Do you magnify your faults as though you are the worst offender, the only one who makes mistakes?

As a believer, you know God forgives you. Now can you forgive yourself? If you continue to dwell on past sins, you are believing Satan's lies. Accepting his whispered accusations can blind you to the truth of God. Yes, it's true, you are imperfect. And yes, God still accepts you and delights in you (Rom. 5:11; Ps. 37:23).

If self-fulfilling prophecy is valid, you can see how important it is to set your mind on God's view of you if you want to feel worthwhile. When you are no longer concentrating on how rotten you are, you can raise your sights even more by helping to build a sense of worth in those close to you. How? By:

- forgiving,
- demonstrating love,
- accepting them as they are,
- respecting them,
- expecting the best from them,
- affirming their value,
- trusting them,
- nurturing their friendship.

FORGIVENESS

It is difficult to forgive others when we ourselves are sinking in a mire of guilt. A lot of false guilt floats around today, but sometimes guilt is necessary and good. Guilt can be positive. An acknowledgment of guilt brings us to confession and the realization of forgiveness. Until we recognize our guilt, there can be no cleansing.

*Sixteen-year-old Jan had come to us from a drug abuse treat-
ment center. While she was there, she had gone through a
self-esteem course in which guilt was viewed as a negative
emotion, always false and always unnecessary. In fact, she was
taught: "We do not make mistakes. We do what we find neces-
sary at any given time and in any given circumstance. Our
actions were right for us at that time. So don't look back; don't
regret the past; don't feel guilty. If others allow themselves to
be hurt by your words or actions, it's their problem, not yours!"*

*Now Jan had deliberately disobeyed us. She repeatedly cited
her reasons for doing so and insisted on vindication. When I
moved beyond the fact of her disobedience and spoke of how
that act had adversely affected others, she said slowly and
accusingly, "It seems to me that you are trying to make me feel
guilty." Exactly!*

At that point, a sense of guilt was appropriate. It was
necessary for Jan to admit to wrongdoing, to feel remorse,
and to experience forgiveness. Without inner cleansing, a
sense of worth is virtually impossible.

Margaret, a senior citizen, wrote us after completing the
self-esteem course:

*My self-esteem was very low. One cause [listed in the course
manual] caught my attention: guilt. I realized the guilt I
needed forgiveness for was an addiction to drugs [prescribed
by several doctors]. . . . From this step [breaking of the addic-
tion], I followed most of the steps to good self-esteem. . . . I was
able to help an older friend [and others] gain better self-esteem
and family relationships. . . .*

How foolish to let guilt rob you of self-worth when the
Bible says so unmistakably that, like Margaret, you can
confess any sin to God and *know* you have forgiveness
(1 John 1:9). You don't have to wait until you have a list of
sins to recite, or until it's bedtime, or until you feel spiritual
enough. Take your sin to him as soon as you are aware of it!

When God forgives, he forgets (Isa. 43:25). King David committed some really grievous sins, yet years later God said to Ahijah: "David . . . kept My commandments and followed Me with all his heart, to do only what was right in My eyes" (1 Kings 14:8, Amp). David had confessed his sins, and God had chosen to forgive and forget them. Like David, you are just as valuable to God after confessing your sin as you were before. So why don't you receive his forgiveness and put your wrongdoing behind you? Stop dwelling on it; forget it as God does. Then check your attitude toward other people. Do you condemn others because they fail to measure up to your standards? You have experienced God's forgiveness; now be as forgiving of others as you need them to be of you.

LOVE

Love is an attitude, not a feeling. Love is active. It involves both your mind and your will, and it takes more than words to communicate. "Have you hugged your kid today?" is a question that challenges us even from car bumpers. Are you expressing your love to those around you?

If 90 percent of your communication of love occurs through nonverbal expressions, you had better mean what your mouth professes so your body can affirm it. Your body language, tone of voice, and facial expression all say more than your words.

Are you having difficulty loving someone? Chances are your attitude toward that person is one of superiority (recognizable by a critical spirit) or inferiority.

- "Can't she see how she turns people off?"
- "Her thoughtless, stupid remarks embarrass me."
- "I'm uncomfortable around him; he's so critical."

It's difficult to genuinely love someone when you feel embarrassed, irritated, or otherwise uncomfortable around him. But those unpleasant feelings are due to *your* attitude.

Freedom to love will come only with freedom from judging.
Vi told us:

For years I had asked God to give me more love for a certain family member. Then one day I realized I should instead ask what sin was standing in the way. He showed me! A superior, critical attitude toward the relative had blocked my love. When I confessed my sin, I was able at last to love that person without reservation the way I had always wanted to.

When God says, "Love covers a multitude of sins" (1 Pet. 4:8, NASB), he doesn't mean you can absolve yourself from sin by loving others. He means that others' sins will not be as visible to you, nor yours to them, if you genuinely love them.

I went home from the self-esteem class and ventured the courage to ask my son what we had done or not done to build his self-worth. He thought a minute and then replied, "I don't remember that you guys had much to do with it—my problems mostly came from my peers. But through everything, I always knew you loved me." I recalled many times when what I'd said and the way I'd acted had blown his self-concept, but he didn't remember that. He remembered the love. I thank God that the deep love he gave me for my children came across to them, even though I was too often critical of them.

Love is the strongest force in the home, most therapists agree. Many therapists say that even if parents use incorrect techniques in raising their children, the children will have a positive home experience if the parents show them loving respect. On the other hand, if all the proper techniques in child-raising are used without love, a negative experience results. God said it all along in the first three verses of 1 Corinthians 13!

ACCEPTANCE

Acceptance is an elusive yet essential ingredient for a sense of worth.

Self-acceptance paves the way for feelings of self-worth. But a person can accept himself only to the degree that he feels accepted by others. And that, of course, is reciprocal.

Can other people, especially family members, say to you, "I love you not only for what you are, but for what I am when I am with you"? Or does your critical attitude cause them to feel unacceptable? Martha shared her experience with us:

My family has wondered why I've not been more loving toward them, and for a long time I didn't know why. Then I realized that every time we were together and one member was absent, we criticized him or her. Though the criticism was masked with concern and sweetened with positive thoughts, I'd come away with negative feelings toward the person. I felt guilty for having joined in, and sure that I was the target when I wasn't there. Because of this, I didn't feel accepted or loved in spite of the togetherness we enjoyed. Nor did I feel the close sense of belonging our family prided itself on. I felt better about myself when I was with friends, so I found myself withdrawing from the family more and more.

When I began to see that my worth depends on God's consistent acceptance and not on others' supposed opinions of me, I realized I didn't need to withdraw from my family. I could stay in there and try to change those cat sessions into accepting fellowship.

It isn't just direct criticism that undermines self-esteem; critical remarks made to you about others also affect your self-worth. Even if you agree with the remarks, you have an uneasy sense that they apply also to you.

An attitude of acceptance is perhaps the most important way counselors can bring about constructive personality growth in a client. You can do the same for those you love.

When we know that others approve of us, we can more easily accept ourselves and be open to change.

RESPECT

Here is a paradox: It is possible to feel accepted but not respected. According to the dictionary, acceptance can be a passive favorable response, whereas respect involves active consideration. Dobson underscores the paradox, explaining that it's easy to show love and disrespect at the same time because love is private while respect has to do with behavior in front of others.[2] You may sincerely *love* the members of your family, but still find it difficult to *respect* them.

Respect is communicated through courteous behavior. Are your family members recipients of your courtesy, or is it reserved for others? Ray Noel hits home when he asks, "What has a stranger ever done for us that we show him courtesy and civility and deny the same to our loved ones?"[3]

A delightful story appeared many years ago in the *Reader's Digest:*

The waitress took the parents' orders, then turned to their small son. "What'll you have?" she asked. "I want a hot dog . . . ," the boy began timidly. "No hot dog," the mother interrupted. "Give him potatoes and beef." But the waitress ignored her. "Do you want ketchup or mustard on your hot dog?" "Ketchup," the boy said with a happy smile, "and a glass of milk." "Coming up," the waitress said, starting for the kitchen. There was a moment of stunned silence. Then the youngster turned to his parents and whispered, "Know what? She thinks I'm real!"

Whether age two or ninety-two, agile or invalid, everyone needs to be treated as "real."

Too often we allow little irritations to quench our respect and blur the best qualities of those we love. We deride and criticize the minor flaws in their characters. Spouses and children are fair game for a sharp tongue or a teasing put-down.

Children especially are easily humiliated in public and in private. They feel disgraced when they are lashed out at in front of others. But in public, many parents are often more concerned with impressing people than with protecting the feelings of their child.

So sometimes we condemn our children for merely acting like children. We may place unrealistic goals on them or, at the other extreme, ignore them, ridicule them, and discourage them from contributing to adult conversation. Other times our disrespect is conveyed by a refusal to give our children the freedom to make a choice—and when they do, heaven help the kids if they make the wrong one!

Donna remembers receiving three pairs of nylon hose for her birthday and wanting to wear them to school. Mother said, "I think you should save them for church, but it's up to you." So Donna made her choice: She wore them to school. And all three pairs disappeared from her drawer that night. Donna says, "We always knew we'd be punished in some way if we didn't choose as she wanted us to." Yet probably that mother would hotly deny that she didn't respect her children's decisions.

Sometimes parents wish to receive respect without giving it. But if you don't respect the dignity of even your smallest child, you can probably expect that he will someday no longer show you the courtesy you now demand. Respect is reciprocal.

For that reason, treating children with respect not only builds their sense of worth but makes the job of training them easier. When you respect your children, they are more likely to respond positively to your requests and rules.

My high school girls were in the kitchen after school, talking over the events of the day with me. When conversation slowed, I said, "I'd appreciate it if one of you would bring the sheets in from the line. And it would be a big help if we could get these dishes out of the sink before I begin supper." I was startled when one daughter said to the other, "Do you notice how Mom always asks us to do something as if we had a choice?" I saw what she meant; this was my usual pattern, and it might even be called dishonest. If it bothered them, I said, I could try to remember in the future to simply ask to have the clothes taken in and the dishes washed. The response: "Oh, no, Mom! Do it the way you always do. It makes us feel good about ourselves."

So periodically check your respect level. When you find occasion to say, "Don't speak to me in that tone of voice," stop for a moment. Your child may well be imitating your tone of voice. Any time you are tempted to give such an order, first stop and listen to yourself.

You see, your children are learning from you how to treat others. They are learning from you how to be kind—or unkind. They learn to show disrespect and discourtesy—or respect and courtesy—according to the way you treat them. How can any parent ignore this fact?

When you overhear your toddler talking into a toy phone or playing with dolls, you may hear yourself speaking. Even your facial expressions may be mirrored in that small face. Does the image you see of yourself in your child embarrass you? Appall you? Like a barometer, those childish, one-way telephone chats can tell us a lot about ourselves. Children model what they see and hear!

Our little girl was playing house with her daddy as he got ready for work—she was Mommy and he was her husband. But when it came time for him to leave, he dropped the role-play and kissed her good-bye with an affectionate, "Be a good girl now." She stiffened and said, with all the force and dignity she could muster, "No! You don't tell mommies, 'Be good.' You say, 'Take it easy today!' " Just what my husband says to me, in all sincerity, every morning.

By your example, you can set the pace for unselfishness—
the very core of courtesy and respect—in your home.

*Our younger children left the table after supper, but my hus-
band and I sat talking, and our teenager remained with us.
After just sitting there silently for perhaps ten minutes or
more, she finally spoke up: "If nobody else wants that last
piece of steak, I'm going to eat it." We asked why she hadn't
eaten it before it grew stone-cold, and she explained: "Well, I
knew that if I asked, Daddy would say he didn't want it even if
he really did. So I had to wait to see."*

EXPECTATIONS

Emerson said, "Our chief want in life is someone who will
make us do what we can." Expecting the best from someone
you love gives him or her a good self-fulfilling prophecy.

Expecting the best doesn't mean you push a person
toward unattainable ideals. It doesn't mean you want your
husband to be the president of his company or your wife to
be a combination of Betty Crocker and Farah Fawcett. It
doesn't mean your son will feel he has let you down because
he isn't a National Merit scholar or a football hero, or that
your daughter must enter a respected profession or the Miss
America contest to fulfill your frustrated dreams.

Expecting the best means you accept others with their
particular aptitudes and limitations and encourage them
right where they are. It doesn't mean you blindly accept all
their actions. It does not preclude correction. It does mean
you stand behind them, helping them reach toward the goal
of being all that God intended them to be. And when we
know others believe in us, we will want to prove them
right! Sarah remembers:

*When our children were preteens, we were amazed to learn
that some of our friends viewed us as the ideal family. We
joked about it at home, but we were deeply honored and
pleased, and each of us became aware of our greater responsi-*

bility to live up to those expectations. My husband and I could tell that our children were proud of our label and didn't want to do anything that would disappoint those admiring friends.

Ken Medema expressed it well:

Love makes great demands, you know. It's curious that love can be demanding and nondemanding at the same time, for we talk about acceptance as a part of love: "I accept you for who you are. I do not condemn you for what you have done. I do not refuse to relate to you no matter where you have been, no matter what your past. Yet, if I love you, I cannot help expecting the best from you. I cannot help wanting you to be what God intended you to be. . . ." So, love is demanding while it is accepting.

When the princesses Elizabeth and Margaret were growing up, it became evident, even at young ages, that each girl was living up to the demands placed on her. Elizabeth was serious, proper, and dignified. Her conduct befitted a future queen. Margaret, in contrast, was fun-loving, mischievous. Hers was the social life-style of normal nobility. Each one had responded to different requirements.

Our future as believers is to reign with the King of kings. As Princess Elizabeth prepared for her reign, so we can live in continuous preparation for ours.

You are made in the image of God. Are you living up to your image? It's an awesome responsibility to live as befits a child of the King. Awesome—but exciting and rewarding!

God expects you to live such a life through his empowerment; he believes you are *worthy* enough for that. Do you recognize your value to him? He shows it by expecting the best of you! You can do the same for others!

AFFIRMATION
Others need to know their worth as much as you do. But why is it so hard to pay a compliment, to affirm another's

good qualities? It's part of the nature of pride. We subconsciously fear that in lifting up someone else we will show ourselves to be less valuable. But the truth is, genuine praise encourages a positive attitude in both of us!

Anne, a college student, urges parents:

Never think you are praising your children too much. They won't get a big head; praise encourages them after all the tearing down they suffer away from home. Praise makes you want to come home because you feel good there. Always find something little to praise them for, but be sure it comes from your heart.

Moms and dads need this reminder often. Remember the survey quoted in chapter one? Even well-intentioned parents give ten put-downs for every one favorable comment!

Anne is right to ask for praise from the heart. If children grow accustomed to flattery, they will doubt sincere affirmation when it comes along.

A currently popular parenting course teaches that children should not be praised because this encourages them to do what is right in order to please others; ideally, they should want to do the right thing from internal motivation. But isn't a desire to please parents the first seed of a desire to please God? We heartily endorse praise as a means of affirmation.

Affirmation is often a matter of attitude. One mother dropped out of our class because she disagreed so strongly with our philosophy of praise and encouragement. She was not about to encourage swelled heads in her children, she said. "They think they're great enough!" was her claim. Sadly, her oldest son, who had a history of behavior problems, was then living in a runaway shelter, determined never to return home.

Another mother reacted quite differently to our views about affirmation:

I came to realize during our class sessions that I haven't been in the habit of affirming my six-year-old son. So last night as I was putting him to bed I told him that I am a very lucky lady. He asked, "Why?" I said, "Because I'm your mommy, and you are a very special boy." This morning he said happily to his daddy, "Mommy is very lucky." "Why?" "Because she's my mommy and I'm special."

What a great thought for a little boy to take through his day!

Or is it? Is that first mother possibly right? Is it unhealthy to tell our children they are special? Will that make them self-centered and proud in a negative sense?

Because Scripture warns against pride, many people conclude that it is wrong and even dangerous to praise others, especially children. But if that is so, then why would God tell us that his people give pleasure to him (Ps. 149:4)? That we even delight him (Ps. 37:23)? Can't we also tell our children that they please and delight us? Can't we even praise them for right attitudes and actions? Surely that kind of affirmation is never inappropriate. No child or adult can receive too much encouragement and honest praise, just as no child or adult can receive too much love.

Your praise, put-downs, and body language communicate your values. Does a beautiful child feel more warmth and acceptance from you than a less attractive one? Does your introverted child feel of less value to you than the one who is a high achiever with personality plus? Does the latter receive more affirmation? We must take great care not to let the good qualities we are striving to build in our children become a measurement of their value in our minds or theirs.

I returned home with Grandma to find the dishes washed and put away. Our ten-year-old was putting the finishing touches on a sparkling-clean kitchen. I expressed my pleasure and appreciation, and Grandma added, "Yes, that's nice; it's the first time I've ever seen you do anything without being asked."

At bedtime a hurting child asked, "Why doesn't Grandma like me?"

Praise given for a job well done could have helped this youngster feel valuable and willing to help again without being asked. But the implied criticism put her focus on her supposed deficiencies instead.

The purpose of affirmation is to build a positive mind-set in another person that frees him from concern with his self-worth so he can center his attention on others. Simple comments we make to others can be timed-release capsules for good—or for bad. When we express appreciation for actions and traits that accentuate God's values, not the world's, we can know it will benefit the hearer.

Recognition of thoughtfulness, honesty, selflessness, helpfulness, trustworthiness, a sense of humor, and wholesome values will help develop those traits. When family members show neatness, cleanliness, and good taste in their appearance, voice your appreciation. If you wish they'd care more about those qualities, you will accomplish far more by acknowledging their slightest attempt than by nagging them about their failure. Your example should encourage the practice of giving compliments. Give compliments privately, if you think they might cause jealousy in another family member with severe esteem problems.

Charlie Shedd speaks of the "warm fuzzies" he and his family like to give each other. A warm fuzzy is something nice someone says about you to encourage you during your day. It's there to remember when you need a boost, reminding you of your worthwhileness when the world around you seems cold and critical.

Affirmation is a warm fuzzy!

TRUST

When I asked my college-bound daughter how we had built her self-esteem, she said without hesitation, "You trusted me." But if we hadn't encouraged her to be dependable from the time she was a toddler, we wouldn't have been able to trust her good judgment as a teenager.

A young mother said of her five-year-old, "I don't trust her; you just can't trust children." Her child fulfilled that negative prophecy and could not be trusted, either as a child or as a teenager. And a child who isn't trustworthy doesn't feel very good about himself.

Norman Wright believes that "a feeling of worthiness is related to a sense of being right and doing right in our eyes and in the eyes of others."[4] If this is true, being trustworthy is crucial to a sense of self-esteem.

The ability to trust yourself is closely related to the trust others place in you. Ask a runner what makes him feel low, and he will probably reply, "Knowing I've broken training." Anyone who is overweight feels the most positive about himself while he is sticking to a diet. You betray your trust in yourself when you don't live up to your best. Self-discipline is the foundation for trustworthiness. Both are essential to a healthy sense of worth. Both can be encouraged in those we love.

FRIENDSHIP

If you're down in the dumps, a letter from a friend, a phone call, or an invitation will renew faith in yourself. All of these affirm your value, and each of us needs that kind of assurance from friends. A good friend will:

- accept you as you are,
- respect you,
- expect the best from you,
- speak well of you,
- guard your confidences.

Friendships require time, and the hours and minutes you invest in your relationships communicate to your friends a sense of worth.

If you wish you had more friends, examine yourself first. When did you last encourage a friendship by giving of your time? Have you been too busy? Is it a case of misplaced values? Are you too concerned with your own needs to care about meeting the needs of others? Robert Briggs said, "Friendship is in loving rather than in being loved."[5] If you reach out in friendship, you'll help others like themselves more, and they will like you more, too!

A favorite saying reads, "A friend is one to whom one may pour out all the contents of one's heart, chaff and grain together, knowing that the gentlest of hands will take and sift it, keep what is worth keeping, and with a breath of kindness, blow the rest away." Could others—even family members—say that about you?

You have that kind of friend. His name is Jesus. He proved, by telling us everything the Father told him, his friendship and our worth (John 15:15). And he laid down his life in the greatest possible demonstration of his love, the ultimate act of friendship! He underscores your worth in many ways:

- He forgives you and removes your guilt.
- He loves you with an everlasting love.
- He accepts you as you are.
- He respects and cherishes you.
- He expects the best of you.
- He values you.
- He trusts you.

Jesus Christ believes in you and affirms your worth. When you do the same for others, you are reflecting him.

QUESTIONS FOR PERSONAL APPLICATION

1. Do you believe in your own worth? Why or why not?
2. Answer each of the questions on pagae 156. If your answer to any question was yes, how can you develop a more positive attitude?

3. Are you experiencing guilt over some sin? Do you fear rejection by God? Is this a valid fear? Read 1 John 1:9. Take your sin to God for cleansing right now.

4. Think of someone close to you in whom you could build a sense of worth. Where will you start?

5. Do your children know you love them? Have you hugged them today? Be sure to demonstrate your love daily.

6. Consider each person you are having difficulty loving. Could the problem be a critical attitude on your part? Do you sense a critical spirit toward you? How can you be accepting and understanding?

7. What do you especially respect about your mate? Have you told him lately? Do so today and then dwell on those positives every day this week. *Always* look for something to respect. Do the same for each of your children.

8. In what ways do you expect the best from your children? In what ways may your demands be too high? Too low?

9. After the names of each of your children, list qualities for which you want to express appreciation. Emphasize godly traits as you daily and privately affirm each child.

10. Do you give more affirmation to one child than to another? What does that tell the other children? What could you begin affirming in those children?

11. Considering the marks of a good friend listed on page 169, could your family members say you are a good friend to them?

12. Has a lack of discipline prevented you from reaching your goals in some area of your life? If this failure causes you to feel bad about yourself, why not begin now to work on your discipline?

QUESTIONS FOR GROUP DISCUSSION

1. Why is achievement alone not enough to give a person a sense of worth?

2. As we seek to affirm our friends and family members for their abilities, how can we also communicate that they are valuable just for being themselves?

3. Does any one of the components of a sense of worth strike you as being more important than the others? Why?

4. Explain this statement: "Love is something you do, not something you feel." What are some of the roadblocks that hinder people from demonstrating love?

5. Do you agree that freedom to love will come only with freedom from judgment? If so, why is this true?

6. How do critical remarks made to you about others affect your self-worth?

7. Why are we more courteous to strangers and friends than to family?

8. In what way is unselfishness the essence of courtesy and respect?

9. In what areas do we need to communicate to our children that we expect the best — but no more than the best—from them?

10. List the most important characteristics that should be displayed in a child of the King of kings. Why would having these expectations for our lives imply worth?

11. What are some "warm fuzzies" we could give each member of our families before they leave the house every morning?

12. Share some unusual ways friendship has been shown to you. What do you see as the characteristics of a good friend?

13. Discuss the relationship of 1 Corinthians 13:1-3 to child-rearing. What actions and abilities does Paul say are meaningless without love?

14 RX: A Sense of Competence
How Capable Are You?

Competence: Gaining a sense of achievement; being affirmed as an able person.[1]

A sense of competence is a sense of adequacy. It is based on the achievement of goals and ideals, and helps us to function in the challenge of coping with life. We are more likely to feel competent if we also enjoy a sense of belonging and worth.

Your sense of competence is healthy when you feel capable and self-confident. It is shored up through:

- receiving parental support,
- receiving peer support,
- doing well in school,
- knowing what to expect in adolescence,
- being realistic about your capabilities,
- accepting responsibility,
- knowing God's evaluation.

PARENTAL SUPPORT

Billy was small for his age and fine-featured like his ninety-eight-pound mother. Bill, Sr., wanted a robust son, and his disappointment was bounced off the boy in subtle ways. Billy couldn't do anything to his father's satisfaction.

Billy stayed with us briefly when he was ten years old. One chaotic day I was preparing to go to the laundromat and he offered his help. I had set a basket of dirty clothes outside the door, and I suggested that he put it into the car for me. Billy went out and came right back to ask, "Which basket?" "It's right outside the door," I said. "The only basket there." He went out again, then opened the door to call, "This basket?" And he came back a third time: "What car should I put it in?" "Our car, Billy, right in front of the house, the only one there. You know our car," I added encouragingly. He took off again, and again he trotted back: "The green car?" And one final trip: "Where should I put it in the car?" I told him to leave it on the grass and we'd put it in the car together.

Billy was an intelligent boy, but the ridicule heaped on him at home made him afraid to turn around for fear he'd rotate in the wrong direction.

Ridicule and sarcasm are ugly, devastating weapons, yet there are parents and teachers and employers who use them as motivational tools. They don't work! They inspire fear and hesitancy, not confidence, so that even placing a basket of clothes in a car can become a major effort, an exhausting exercise. If you fear failure, any situation can pose a threat and become an occasion for anxiety.

A supportive, encouraging atmosphere, on the other hand, is strongly conducive to achievement. A school psychologist contends that children are born with a certain potential, but whether or not they develop it depends on the family in which they are raised. Dr. Neil Solomon said in his syndicated column:

While educators and mental health professionals, in general, have been aware for some time of the importance of parent-child relationships in stimulating intellectual curiosity and developing a desire for knowledge, a recent study has added support to the theory. The findings of this survey indicate that children who are held, talked to, and praised tend to develop intellectually more rapidly than children who do not receive as much warmth and affection.[2]

Strong parental love, continuously reinforced, certainly helps to develop a child's sense of competence. But will it provide enough self-confidence to counteract all the negatives thrown at him every day away from the safety of the nest?

Unfortunately, no. Self-confidence that has been developed at home through sensitive parenting can be shattered on the playground.

PEER SUPPORT

Acceptance by peers means everything during the school years, especially during the early and middle teens.

I had both an excellent record and strong parental support, and most of my teachers liked me.

Actually, I had three sets of boosters: teachers, parents, and church family. (Some people have none of these.) According to the experts, I should have been on top of the world. But even with all those strengths, I had a bottom-of-the-heap image of myself when I was with my peers at school. I felt the agony of shyness and self-consciousness.

All my strengths didn't shield me from a school humiliation that still comes vividly to mind: I was excluded by the selection method. In a spelldown I'd have been selected early because of my ability. But when a party was planned, popularity became the key to the choice. A boy who was popular and self-confident (usually synonymous) invited all the eighth-grade boys to his party, and each was to invite a girl from the class. But there weren't enough boys to go around. The agony was in the waiting for a boy to ask me, and when the last day finalized the unthinkable, unacceptable, and yet unmistakable verdict, I could only hope that my parents and siblings would never hear of that great eighth-grade party and ask why I hadn't gone.

Experiences like that one cast an inferiority complex in concrete, ravaging any vestige of self-confidence. Unless peers allow you to feel that you matter, your other strengths won't uphold you during those adolescent years. Achievement in the classroom and affirmation at home are not enough if classmates and coworkers don't extend equal approval. A downward spiral can develop until maturity intervenes. And for some people it never changes.

An inferiority complex builds a wall that most people won't try to penetrate because they are hiding behind their own defenses. If your self-focus is intense, you scare others off and prevent them from encouraging your sense of competence. Follow up the story of the eighth-grade party:

Ninth grade found me in a new school district, in a huge high school among strangers. Knowing that the laughing groups around me wouldn't be interested in me—indeed, that no one who mattered would have any interest in me—I kept to myself, living a lonely existence in the crowd.

My English teacher liked my writing. She often read my compositions aloud and gave me the top grade on everything I wrote for her. One homework assignment required two people to collaborate on a radio commercial, and she left the pairing-off to us. Since no one approached me, I solved the problem by staying home sick and turning in a late solo effort.

It never occurred to me that anyone might be waiting and hoping to be approached by me in order to get a better grade. It never occurred to me that my aloneness could be considered aloofness. (I needed someone to tell me that!) I would never have believed that lesser scholars might be intimidated by me, even as I was intimidated by their popularity, their appearance, their camaraderie.

It was nice to be appreciated by my teachers, but to be liked by my peers and accepted into their close-knit groups would have meant far more.

There were some schoolmates with whom I could be friendly because they obviously needed me as much as I needed them— poor students with a kindred sense of inferiority. They clung to me and looked up to me, and I was grateful. Perhaps I pitied them and enjoyed feeling superior, yet I also empathized with them. How could I not? But their admiration did nothing to enhance my self-confidence when I was around the "in" groups—my followers were even further outside the magic circle than I.

We can be self-confident wherever we feel accepted. So we may have a sense of competence in one group, yet feel totally useless in another. Peer support during those sometimes fearful school years is as crucial to self-confidence as a supportive climate at home. Parents, show sensitivity to your child's needs for close friendships during this time!

ACADEMIC SUCCESS

Academic excellence is definitely not the first priority of most high school students, but it matters a great deal to children in their early school years. School can be harrowing if it is a struggle to keep up with classmates, if peers are reading more easily and grasping the basics of math that leave you bewildered, or if you are placed in that unfortunate classification of slow learner.

Perhaps the most constructive approach parents can take to report cards is to keep them private. No child should have to compete with his siblings; there is enough competition in the classroom! Certainly, we need to provide incentives for our children; like anyone else, they need help if they're to stretch to their potential. They may be capable of far more than they realize and only need encouragement.

But if they really can't make the grade, they won't benefit from comparison with others. Each person does enough of that on his own anyway. The additional comparisons may convince him he is slower than he really is.

Polly was a gifted student. Sister Patty, one year younger, was of average ability and far more shy and reserved. Imagine the effect on Patty's sense of competence when, on the first day of fifth grade, a teacher who demanded the most from her students asked for a written account of summer vacation and singled out Patty: "If you're anything like your sister, I know I'll get a good story from you." Zap! Shot down on day one.

Says Dr. James Dobson, children "face failure as a daily routine in the classroom. . . . One-fourth to one-half of our children will eventually enter adult life having had twelve years' experience in feeling dumb."[3]

Sometimes a slow learner is really just a late bloomer who was pushed into school before he was ready. Unfortunately, age rather than development usually determines when a child enrolls in school, and many parents are embarrassed to admit that a child is not mature enough. How's that for false pride! A young mother in our self-esteem class confessed:

I was the youngest in my class all through school, and it was a point of distinction and pride for me and my parents. So it was hard for me to accept the advice that my daughter should wait another year before beginning school. Only when I recognized through your class that my pride was involved was I able to agree on the best course for my child. I'm thankful I didn't make her struggle to keep up by pushing her into school with her age group.

REALISTIC EXPECTATIONS OF ADOLESCENTS

A sense of competence seems to be particularly elusive during the teen years. In *Hide or Seek,* Dobson urges that children be prepared well in advance for the heartaches of adolescence. Your children should know they are going to experience a self-worth crisis during the vulnerable junior high years, a crisis that will affect their sense of competency. Though it's probably a temporary condition, a short-term disease, it can be a painful one. The process of becoming an adult makes you unsure of yourself; it's the nature of adolescent years to feel incompetent.

Even cheerleaders and beauty queens and sports heroes suffer from self-doubt. Jane was a vivacious, attractive, popular cheerleader from a loving and wealthy home, with the clothes sense to take full advantage of her expensive wardrobe. Yet she now claims, "I was always scared in school." (She wasn't an A+ scholar.)

Self-doubt may be the universal adolescent malady—but your child still needs prior warning. If he knows where the pain is likely to occur, he can build defenses against it, counsels Dobson. He or she needs to know that everyone feels clumsy and incompetent and stupid sometimes, just as he does. High school years are full of experimentation, of soundings for areas of strength. Mistakes and embarrassing moments are a part of the learning process; they go with the territory.

Tell your child in advance some of the changes that will be taking place in him or her. Physical growth will bring fluctuating emotions and sometimes bewildering moods. New fears, responsibilities, temptations—and more opportunities to goof will also accompany adolescence.

In addition to other changes, most teenagers experience spiritual confusion. Stressful questioning and soul-searching are a normal and perhaps necessary part of growing up. Be ready to field challenges to your faith in an accepting manner.

Another difficult adjustment for both you and your child will occur due to your child's mushrooming need for independence. As children spread their wings and begin to question their parents' authority, thrusting out further from home in search for their own answers, distance can develop between the two generations. Sometimes the trust that once existed in the parent-child relationship is shaken, leaving both parties bewildered and resentful.

So children and parents all need preparation for puberty. Without it, feelings of inadequacy and self-doubt can seem overwhelming to a teenager. Just having intimate talks with parents about what to anticipate during adolescence will boost a child's self-confidence.

A parent can take two steps while his child is still young to help ease the transition into adolescence. The first is to equip him with training in polite behavior and correct manners. Teach your child social skills—how to be gracious, how to do things correctly, what words to say—if you want him to feel competent as a teenager. Everyone feels inadequate when they don't know what's expected of them— even if it's just not knowing which fork to use!

Our teenage daughter returned from an errand and shared the following experience: "That man thought I was so polite; he told me several times how much he appreciated it. Mom, I wasn't trying to be polite. I wasn't even aware of having said 'please' or 'thanks.' I'm so glad you taught us that way, so it just comes naturally and we can be polite without even thinking about it."

And perhaps, from early childhood, you could prepare your child for adolescence in another way: by helping him be aware of the self-esteem needs of others. "Why do you think your friend keeps his eyes lowered and his head down?" you might ask your child. The more he can recognize others' self-image problems, the less preoccupied he will be with his own. His concern for others will help him to reach out, which will develop his self-confidence.

Talk about the importance of self-confidence even in his earliest years. Convince him that he likes himself! Children need to be taught from early childhood, as a habit, to lift their heads, to look others in the eye, to feel good about themselves. Not to be proud, but to feel equal. To enjoy being who they are.

And adults can learn to do the same!

REALISTIC SELF-APPRAISAL

Perfectionism, a preoccupation with flawless behavior, can erode your sense of competence. Perfectionism can be painful, like a gremlin that sits on your shoulder and ties your wings, bogging you down in details and dissatisfaction. Being a perfectionist is like standing at a window with a breathtaking view of mountain, lake, and forest, and seeing only the smudge on the windowpane.

You can flog yourself for the rest of your life, but you still will never attain perfect job performance, a perfect marriage, perfect parenthood, or perfect spirituality. No matter how you strain, you'll never make it.

Even as Christians, we will never be perfectly mature. Paul calls all Christians saints, but God knows we're not yet saintly! And if you put more mature Christians on a pedestal, expecting saintliness from them, you're doomed to disappointment. They're bound to topple sometime, and you may be crushed in the fall.

Visiting friends were complaining about our pastor, and their remarks were critical and unkind. We tried to soothe the friends and yet defend our pastor, hoping the children were asleep and unhearing. But later, when I went to check on them, I found our sensitive thirteen-year-old still awake—and weeping. A child who demanded perfection of herself, she felt she could never measure up, that she always failed in what God expected of her. All she could say was, "I thought the older I got the easier it would be, but if people who have been Christians for that long can still be so critical, what hope is there for me?"

Perfectionism can be a strong, positive motivator, but it is usually unrealistic. It can keep you miserable and make your family, friends, and coworkers uncomfortable. If nobody measures up to your standards, then that includes you—but others don't understand that. Your critical attitude is all they can see, and they are too busy resenting it to be aware of your problems with yourself.

Your high expectations are easily passed on to your children, who soon learn they should be perfect, too. At its extreme, perfectionism can become emotional abuse:

In the case of Susan, the outside world perceives a seemingly well-adjusted child, unaware of the intense pressure she experiences in striving to meet the unreasonably high demands her parents have established for her. . . . Even when she does well, her parents are adept at locating other areas for criticism, and thus Susan feels that most of her accomplishments are not "good enough." . . . Undertakings that do not achieve perfect results are viewed as failures. Such occurrences indicate to Susan that she is an inadequate person, unworthy of the love of others. Even as adults, individuals raised in emotionally abusive environments carry these distorted perceptions with them.

Making decisions is especially painful because of fear that making a choice will result in less than perfect consequences. Unreasonably high expectations create enormous pressure and anxiety. . . . Not uncommonly, men and women who were emotionally abused [early in life] unintentionally repeat this "anticipation of excellence" when raising their own children.[4]

No one is perfect in every area, but everyone is competent in some areas. You need to praise God for these areas of strength in your life. Surely you need to stretch toward your potential, but you need also to recognize your limitations and accept them *thankfully.* More praising and less fretting would do wonders for your sense of competence! And it would encourage others, as well!

RESPONSIBILITY

A university chaplain believes one of the reasons people join cults is to release them from responsibility for their actions. If you haven't been *taught* to be responsible, you won't feel able to handle responsibility. You'll naturally seek a nest to hide in.

Parents can fail to teach accountability either through neglect or through overprotection. Neglectful parenting doesn't call a child to account for his actions, and over-protectiveness shields him from their consequences. Training in responsibility—or irresponsibility—begins in early childhood. An overprotective attitude communicates that it's a big, bad world out there and you can't handle it alone. Protective parents strongly identify with everything their children do and try to control their responses. "You need us to take care of you" is their message, which either stifles self-confidence or encourages rebellion. In both ways, overprotection spawns insecurity.

Parental confidence in a child's ability and judgment is vital to his development; a child needs his parents to communicate that he *is* adequate, that he *can* do it, that he *is* capable.

I asked our high achiever in what ways we helped to develop her self-confidence. Her response was immediate. "Well, the most important thing, of course, was that you always respected my opinion. And then there was your confidence in me: You seemed to just assume I would do the right thing."

Now obviously we didn't always respect her opinions! Sometimes they amused us or irritated us or worried us. And sometimes our confidence was misplaced. But I'm thankful she felt our trust and our respect.

Even with that kind of support, no one—child, adolescent, or adult—will ever feel competent until he begins taking responsibility for his actions and stops blaming others for his mistakes. He must begin to clean up his own debris and stop waiting for others to straighten things out for him.

Parents can teach responsibility through assigned tasks within a child's capabilities and correctly instructing him when he fails. Consequently, he learns if he spills his milk, he can get a cloth and help clean it up; if he smashes a toy, it was his choice and his toy won't be replaced. If he loses a friend through selfishness or unkindness, it was his decision; if he fails a test he didn't study for, it's not the teacher's fault for asking hard questions; if he runs out of gas, it's not the fault of his parents or the car.

Any time a child ignores clear rules and instruction, the consequences are, again, his own choice. Not his parents', his teacher's, his employer's, the government's, his friend's, or his enemy's. His.

GOD'S EVALUATION

So you make a lot of mistakes? You goof? You foul things up?

God says he can take all of your mistakes and failures and turn them around: "And we know that in all things God works for the good of those who love him, who have been called according to his purpose" (Rom. 8:28, NIV).

So even when you blow it, God can use your mistakes for your growth and for his glory. He never yells, "If I've told you once, I've told you a thousand times; don't you ever listen?" He just repeats the lessons over and over and over again. He builds your sense of competence with patience; he understands you are still in the process of maturing. It's as though when he looks down on you he sees the popular button that reads: PBPGINFWMY! (Please Be Patient: God Is Not Finished With Me Yet!).

We still have so much to learn, and he has so much to do to change us into his likeness, but he takes the responsibility for the finished product: "Being confident of this, that he who began a good work in you will carry it on to completion until the day of Christ Jesus" (Phil. 1:6, NIV).

If your heavenly Father is taking care of the process of transforming you into his image, that leaves you free to go about your business, the business of making him known where he has put you. He has appointed you to be an ambassador—to represent him to the people of your world. He thinks you are capable!

You see, *he knows you are competent for the job because he equips you with everything you need to accomplish it.* He gives you access to his wisdom and his ability, and he'll even love people through you. He'll be the genesis of all your activity if you let him. But if your effort originates with you, it's impotent; you will only be flapping your wings.

He will empower you. He will make you competent.

QUESTIONS FOR PERSONAL APPLICATION

1. What were some areas of self-doubt in your adolescent years? Have you overcome them? If so, how? If not, how do they affect you now?
2. What school experiences may have negatively affected your children's self-images? Can they somehow be turned around and used for good in their lives?
3. Reflect on your own adolescence. Would prior discussion have helped you deal with the changes you experienced?
4. What is your response when your children goof? How might your attitude make a difference in their willingness to learn through trial and error?
5. Are you a perfectionist in any area? In what ways could that be undermining your self-esteem? Your children's?
6. How are you training your children to be responsible? What changes do you need to make? How can you implement those changes so your children will accept them?
7. Do you accept responsibility for your mistakes and sins or do you tend to justify yourself and put the blame elsewhere?
8. Do you demonstrate respect for the opinions of your mate and children?
9. In what areas has God made you competent? How might you use these gifts and abilities as his ambassador?
10. Put into your own words Philippians 1:6: "Being confident of this, that he who began a good work in you will carry it on to completion until the day of Christ Jesus."

QUESTIONS FOR GROUP DISCUSSION

1. In what ways can we build a sense of competence in our children? In what ways do we undermine it?
2. Which do you think is more important to an adolescent's sense of competence: parental affirmation or peer support? Why?
3. How might you encourage a child who is not readily accepted by his peers?
4. List warnings you could give your adolescent children to lessen feelings of self-doubt and incompetence.
5. In what ways can you help your children develop self-confidence and enjoy being who they are?
6. What are some of the dangers inherent in perfectionism?
7. How can a perfectionist work on developing more realistic standards and accepting imperfections within himself and others?
8. What are some specific tasks that can be assigned to children at various ages to teach them responsibility?
9. Think of a time when you felt especially good about yourself. Who or what was responsible? Recall a time when you felt incompetent. Could someone have helped you? How?
10. Discuss why Philippians 1:6 bolsters a Christian's sense of competence.

15 I Need a Specialist
Special Challenges to Self-Esteem

Ideally, all three segments of self-esteem—belonging, worth, and competence—will be equally present in a person's life:

- You'll belong to some kind of group.
- You'll have the inner assurance that you are a valuable person.
- You'll feel competent to perform the necessary functions of life.

But life is seldom ideal. Can strength in one or two of the components of self-esteem make up for a deficiency in the others?

Improving any aspect of self-esteem takes determination and motivation. You can make the effort to belong somewhere by joining a group and instigating friendships within that group. You can feel more competent by diligently applying yourself to learning new skills. But to bolster a sense of worth requires the greatest strength of all—changing what you tell yourself about your value.

A sense of belonging comes from interaction with others; a sense of competence comes from what you do; but a sense of worth is controlled by your thoughts. The more difficult the circumstances of your life, the more intense will be your struggle for assurance. Certain conditions create special needs for reinforcement in all three areas. What are some of these conditions?

A SHAKY MARRIAGE

We have already seen how emotional deprivation at home can harm a child's self-esteem. By adolescence, when feelings of worth and competence are most unstable, a child who has lacked nurturance may develop an overwhelming ache to be the most important person in the world to someone else. Deep, unmet esteem needs make teenagers especially susceptible to sexual attraction and the pressure to conform.

Being left out is one of the greatest fears of an adolescent. Like going steady, being married assures one of a partner— only on a more solid basis—and that benefit forms the unfortunate foundation of many marriages. Too many weddings occur simply because of an overriding need for affirmation. Because each of us wants to be "number one" to someone else, we fall in love with the one who thinks we are attractive, the one who picks us over the others. And so two people embark on a supposedly lifelong commitment.

What an uncertain basis for a marriage! What happens when sexual attraction wears off? When we fall out of love? Our unhealthy self-esteem is laid bare. We begin to nitpick, gripe, degrade, humiliate, or, worst of all, ignore the other person. We major on the minors, slowly whittling away the foundation of each other's self-esteem.

As our frustration builds and boils over, we may spew out ugly words that cause deep damage to our spouse. "You make a lousy mother!" "If you'd get a decent job, you could quit nagging about how much I spend!" "I wonder what I ever saw in you!" "I can hardly stand to be around you anymore!" More subtle or sarcastic jabs may cut even deeper.

A marriage built only on esteem needs and sexual attraction rests on a shaky foundation. The affirmation that was once given by your partner can be found in other ways. Perhaps you become successful in your career, and as your self-respect rises, your respect for your mate falls. Or someone else is attracted to you, and the boost to your ego catches you up and frees your inhibitions. The esteem you once gave to the one you married is transferred to a new love, and self-centeredness makes you insensitive to the pain you are inflicting.

Unmet esteem needs can spoil a marriage unless you deliberately choose to be more concerned with meeting the needs of your partner than in getting what you think you deserve.

"Do nothing from selfishness or empty conceit, but with humility of mind let each of you regard one another as more important than himself; do not merely look out for your own personal interests, but also for the interests of others" (Phil. 2:3-4, NASB).

After reading these verses, Kathy knew what kind of commitment God was asking of her, and she struggled with the challenge for a long time. I watched as tears streamed down her face in silent testimony to the battle going on inside. After what seemed an interminable silence, Kathy prayed, determining to put her husband's needs above her own.

It wouldn't be easy. For too long Kathy had been the attacker, sending her husband more and more into his stubborn, silent, defensive shell, a protection that was both an inherent part of his personality and a product of his upbringing. The more he withdrew, the more she verbally abused him. Now she understood why he had not made love to her in more than two years.

After Kathy's prayer of commitment, her radiance showed the release she had experienced. Her attitude toward her husband changed so quickly that by the end of the first day he said, "I don't know what she told you, but I like the change in you!" And he began again to demonstrate his love for her in his quiet way.

It has been difficult for Kathy to walk in her husband's moccasins and try to understand his feelings and his needs. And it will be a conscious choice she will struggle to implement for a long time to come. But it's worth it. It has saved and enhanced their marriage.

Even an already good marriage takes commitment. How much more is required of one that is struggling. Yet the rewards of a healthy relationship far outweigh its costs!

If both partners are not committed to building up each other, the bitter road toward divorce is closer than they realize. Probably the greatest loss felt in a divorce is that of self-esteem. After a divorce, you no longer have a sense of belonging to a marriage partner. Your failure to have a happy relationship degrades your sense of competence. So the conclusion many divorced people draw is "I am now less valuable than I was before my divorce."

You need a healthy self-esteem when you enter marriage so you'll be able to see yourself and your partner realistically. When you feel equal to each other before you marry, you can just be grateful for the additional belonging, worth, and sense of competence the union brings you. You'll even have more desire to meet the needs of your spouse than to have him or her meet your own. What healing such a marriage can bring to wounds of the past!

SINGLENESS

But consider the unmarried. Needs for close family support must be met elsewhere, and for some, the void is never adequately filled. Many formerly married people have support groups, and others have young children to whom they are still the most important person in the world. Those close relationships temper the poor self-concept that can result from a failed marriage.

The single who has never before married is perhaps more

vulnerable to unhealthy self-esteem. If low self-esteem and depression are rampant even among happily married women, how far-reaching are they among the never-married? The singles among us need to be included—as everyone does—in our range of acceptance and appreciation.

LOSS AND AGING

The death of a mate also leaves a great void, especially after years of the self-esteem reinforcement inherent in a strong supportive marriage. Feelings of belonging will be shattered, and the assurance of worth and competence may be damaged for a time. Sometimes self-esteem is never fully regained.

Any substantial loss—a relationship, a home, a job—can create the same effect. Since a sure fact of growing older is that losses begin to outnumber gains, it's easy to see that by the time we are considered elderly, our areas of strength may be whittled down so far that our self-concept is in serious trouble.

Most residents of nursing homes have lost all three elements of their self-esteem—belonging, worth, and competence. Many have no family nearby. Others have families who take little time for them. They are unable to stay in their own homes or even to care for their most basic needs, and they are no longer considered of value to our society. Even the aged who are able to care for themselves can easily feel useless and unproductive. Children and grandchildren are too busy for them, and often they feel as though they are on the outside of life looking in. It seems they are no longer needed by the impatient young.

Poet Shel Silverstein captures the older person's dilemma perfectly:

Said the little boy, "Sometimes I drop my spoon."
Said the little old man, "I do that too."
The little boy whispered, "I wet my pants."

"I do that too," laughed the little old man.
Said the little boy, "I often cry."
The old man nodded, "So do I."
"But worst of all," said the boy, "it seems
Grown-ups don't pay attention to me."
And he felt the warmth of a wrinkled old hand.
"I know what you mean," said the little old man.[1]

How can the aged regain a sense of worth? Their experience and their insight and their painfully gained know-how are invaluable—a source of wisdom often tragically untapped. Some of the elderly meet their esteem needs by reaching out to the hurting, the handicapped, and the lonely, thereby assuaging their own loneliness. It is essential to feel useful, even when it is impossible to match past achievements.

DISABILITY

For the handicapped, a solid sense of belonging is absolutely crucial. Without the acceptance of others, a disabled person's sense of incompetence can destroy his self-worth. Some handicapped people are able to perform compensatory tasks, abilities often gained with much difficulty, but others are unable to feel competent at *any* level. Not everyone has the latent talents of a Joni Eareckson Tada, or the great support team that has helped her to use them.

The best gift we can give to the disabled is the assurance that they *belong,* that they have a place. They, perhaps more than anyone else, need to know we accept them as they are, love them for who they are, and want to include them in our circle no matter what their limitations.

LASTING STABILITY

Circumstances—even the length of our days on earth—are uncertain. Any of us may face the emptiness of life in a nursing home. If our sense of belonging, worth, and competence is based only on the world's values, we will never be secure. We risk battles for our self-esteem whenever life's reversals occur.

The only constant, never-ending source of self-esteem is found in God, and nothing can take him from you. Not dismissal from your job, the loss of your home and possessions, the destruction of your marriage, the death of loved ones, or the daily grind of existence in a care center. When your sense of belonging, worth, and competence are based on eternal truths, they won't fade with age or be crushed by the circumstances of life.

Using an analogy of Waylon Ward's, we see that self-esteem rests on three pillars—belonging, worth, and competence. The triune God is the only foundation that can keep them from sinking. God himself has provided the means through which our self-esteem needs are met.

SELF-ESTEEM

Belonging | Worth | Competence

God the Father | God the Son | God the Holy Spirit

- *God the Father adopted us:* We *belong* in his family. "His unchanging plan has always been to adopt us into his own family by sending Jesus Christ to die for us. And he did this because he wanted to!" (Eph. 1:5, TLB).
- *God the Son died for us:* We are *worth* the price he paid. "But [you were purchased] with the precious blood of Christ the Messiah" (1 Pet. 1:19, Amp).

- *God the Holy Spirit empowers us:* We become *competent* through him. "But you shall receive power—ability, efficiency and might—when the Holy Spirit has come upon you" (Acts 1:8, Amp).

  Regardless of our circumstances, almighty God can lift our self-esteem to the highest possible position of health and well-being. We need to dwell on his provision instead of our lack. Our ultimate strength is the sure knowledge that God exists and cares!

QUESTIONS FOR PERSONAL APPLICATION

1. Which dimension of self-esteem—belonging, worth, or competence—is most lacking in your life?
2. Which dimension is strongest? How might you use that strength to help others achieve healthy self-esteem?
3. In which of the three areas of esteem does your family need the most improvement? What changes will you implement over the next six months to meet this need? What changes will you begin this week? What can you do to improve the other two dimensions of esteem as well?
4. Do your family members or friends have any of the special esteem needs referred to in this chapter? What can you do to help meet those needs?
5. In what sincere ways can you double your reinforcement of your teen's belonging, worth, and competence while still respecting his need to become independent? Be specific according to the particular needs of each of your children.
6. In what way and to what extent have your unmet esteem needs harmed your marriage?
7. No matter how much your mate has hurt you, could it be that you are selfish in your relationship? In what ways? How are you hurting your mate with words—or the lack of them—and with actions—or the lack of them?
8. Are you, like Kathy, willing to obey Philippians 2:3-4 by being more concerned about your mate's needs and interests than your own? Would you make a commitment to God to reread this passage and renew your goal every morning for several weeks or months? Who could you ask to hold you accountable?
9. In a special family meeting, brainstorm ways of building belonging, worth, and competence in elderly parents, grandparents, and friends. Design projects you can do together weekly, biweekly, or monthly to meet those special needs.

10. On what foundation does your self-esteem rest? On the shifting sands of public opinion? Or on God?

QUESTIONS FOR GROUP DISCUSSION

1. Brainstorm ways we build belonging, worth, and competence in our mates and how we tear them down. (If you are in a couple's class, divide into groups of men and women. Record your ideas, then share them with the whole group.)
2. In what ways is a sense of worth dependent on a sense of belonging? On a sense of competence?
3. Why do teenagers have a special need for belonging, worth, and competence?
4. Would you agree that many weddings occur because of esteem needs? In what ways might unmet esteem needs harm a marriage?
5. Why would entering a marriage with healthy self-esteem make a difference in the quality of that marriage?
6. Discuss what changes you think may have taken place in Kathy when she began to apply Philippians 2:3-4 to her marriage.
7. What specific steps could one take to put his partner's needs above his own?
8. The assurance of belonging, worth, and competence can be severely shaken due to divorce. What could you do to help a friend undergoing such trauma?
9. Do you think couples tend to exclude singles from their fellowship? Do singles do the same to couples? What can you do about it?
10. How can we impart to elderly people a sense of worthwhileness, a sense of being needed?
11. Explain the saying, "Life's heaviest burden is not having anything to carry."
12. How can we help the handicapped people we know develop a deeper sense of belonging, worth, and competence?

16   Preventive Care for Your Home
Discipline and Your Child's Self-Esteem

Remember the story of the boy who didn't want to finish his supper? His nanny dourly assured him that it makes God angry when we waste food. After supper a good storm blew up, and the boy stood at the window with hands clasped behind his back, his small shoulders hunched, watching the lightning flash and the trees bend in the wind. The fierce rumble of thunder filled the room, and the boy slowly shook his head: "Such a fuss over two prunes!"

How many children could say the same thing about the correction they receive? No wonder the word *discipline* usually elicits a negative reaction. A youth worker tells us that one of the greatest problems he deals with in the teenagers he counsels is the effect of unwise discipline. Too often discipline tears down the self-esteem of a child rather than building it up. It damages instead of nurtures. But the right kind of discipline is a major factor in the prevention of unhealthy self-esteem.

WHAT IS DISCIPLINE?
Before we discuss the subject of discipline, let's define what we mean by the term.

First, remove the concept of harsh retaliation from your mind. Discipline is *not* synonymous with punishment. Its purpose, focus, and attitude all differ:

- to punish is to penalize, looking back in anger and frustration.
- to discipline is to train, looking forward in love and concern.

The result in a child is very different, also! Punishment often leads to fear, guilt, hostility, rebellion, resentment, and poor self-esteem. Discipline gives a sense of security and encourages self-reliance, self-control, initiative, contentment, and healthy self-esteem.

We like Brandt and Dowdy's definition of discipline:

To discipline [a child] is not to punish him for stepping out of line, but to teach that child the way he ought to go. Discipline, therefore, includes everything that you do to help your children learn.[1]

Since discipline includes everything you do to disciple or train your children, it is important that you know not only how to correct them appropriately, but also how to minimize and even prevent the need for correction. Preventive steps include:

- providing support and guidance
- meeting basic needs
- establishing reasonable rules
- correcting carefully and wisely.

SUPPORT AND GUIDANCE

Some parents are as demanding as drill sergeants. At the other end of the spectrum, some establish no firm rules at all.

Parents fall into four general categories, according to the National Council on Family Relations that met in 1971. The results of the council's study, which are charted below, show that parents who mix strong love with strong guidelines provide their children with the highest self-esteem. These findings are affirmed in other studies.

Type of Parenting	Support and Affirmation	Control and Guidance	Child's Self-Esteem
Authoritative	High	High	Most healthy
Permissive	High	Low	Second healthiest
Authoritarian	Low	High	Lower
Neglectful	Low	Low	Lowest

The study also documents that parents who fall into the last two categories, offering little love and support and either too much control or none at all, most often produce children who identify with a counterculture such as a gang or a cult.[2]

When a child grows up without behavioral boundaries, he misses the opportunity to learn self-control, marring his effectiveness as an adult. If children don't learn how to control themselves, they will fall prey as adults to the worries, fears, angers, and desires that characterized their early years.

A child learns the meaning of self-control by responding to authorities in his life. That knowledge usually begins when he is very young. For the sake of their child, parents must establish their authority.

However the inability to be firm is one of the most common problems of parents today. The lack of self-assurance felt by many parents is reflected in the question asked of a newspaper columnist: "If I insist on strict obedience, won't I lose my children's devotion?"

The columnist who responded to this question cited the

example of her husband. Her children love and respect him because they know he'll discipline them when they disobey. Her observation confirms the findings of the 1971 National Council Study: When parents exert loving control over their children, children are most apt to have positive feelings about themselves and about those in authority over them. They are less prone to destructive rebellion than other children, and are even more likely to follow their parents' religious beliefs.[3]

Obedience is important to God. The New Testament twice catalogs behavioral characteristics of evil people. Both lists include disobedience to parents (Rom. 1:30; 2 Tim. 3:2).

God expects parents to train their children to obey, and he shows us how to do it: "I will be a father to him and he will be a son to Me; when he commits iniquity, I will correct him . . . but My lovingkindness shall not depart from him" (2 Sam. 7:14-15, NASB).

Correction with lovingkindness—God mirrors the perfect authoritative parent. A. W. Tozer expands on this aspect of God's character in *The Knowledge of the Holy:*

The familiar picture of God as often torn between His justice and His mercy is altogether false. . . . There is nothing in His justice which forbids the exercise of His mercy. . . . God is never at cross purposes with Himself. No attribute of God is in conflict with another. God's compassion flows out of His goodness, and goodness without justice is not goodness.[4]

In other words, God's character does not change because we sin. He doesn't set aside his kindness or his holiness because he is angry over our disobedience. He doesn't indicate that he has had it with us, even when we grieve him. He doesn't punish us vindictively, but he disciplines us for our good, that we might become more godly (Heb. 12:10). His faithfulness, compassion, and long-suffering remain constant, even when *our* faithfulness falters or disappears.

These same attitudes are the ones godly parents strive for,

not only when their children act angelic, but also when they disobey. As God works in our lives, our parenting will bear evidence of the fruits of his Spirit (Gal. 5:22-23), regardless of our children's response to us.

An effective authoritative parent is one who sets the example by his own behavior. He shows respect for his children, even as he corrects them. He is honest enough to admit mistakes and ask forgiveness of his children when necessary. He earnestly tries to be fair and consistent in all of his interactions with his family, even though consistency is probably the most elusive ingredient of good parenting. He responds to the needs of his family even when it means self-sacrifice. He is open to changes he needs to make in himself and his parenting. He shows understanding and flexibility, yet he is not afraid to stand up and take control. He provides the moral strength and leadership his family needs in an age of conflict and turmoil.

This is the authoritative parent at his best. He may sound like Superdad in Utopia, but God can enable each of us to follow this pattern and reach these goals.

MEET BASIC NEEDS

Godly, authoritative parenting will minimize the need for correction. A top priority in this kind of parenting is meeting your child's basic needs—food, rest, a healthy environment, love, and security. In fact, one writer states emphatically that three-quarters of a child's behavioral problems can be solved by meeting his basic needs.[5]

Try to anticipate these needs rather than waiting until they are manifested in an inappropriate manner. When unmet needs result in unacceptable behavior, exercise more understanding and less correction than you would under other circumstances. If your child is misbehaving before mealtime, it's probably because he's hungry; an early dinner or a nutritious late-afternoon snack might forestall an explosion. If he missed his nap or didn't get enough sleep the night before, don't come down hard on him; he's acting up because he's tired and doesn't know how to handle his frustration.

Consider what other circumstances may be affecting your child's behavior. Perhaps he's coming down with the flu, or he's tense over an upcoming exam or recital. Perhaps he needs to talk about something that's bothering him but doesn't know how to bring it up. It could be that he's confused about your rules: You haven't made them clear, or you've failed to enforce them consistently. Or maybe it's just your impatient attitude, your preoccupation with that overwhelming to-do list that's bothering him. Your tenseness will affect your child's behavior. It may make him anxious and easily angered.

A young woman who had been in our home several times remarked one day, "It's so different over here. You don't feel tension in the air. Everyone isn't always on each other's backs around here."

Some needs go unmet in almost every home almost every day. Parents must exercise patience as they teach their children to cope with life's frustrations. Whatever your child's needs, you are the one who must care enough to help him sort them out, persistently helping him to become the person he can be.

Our fifth grader was behaving obnoxiously, and the problem seemed to worsen every day. There was no pleasing him, and he often took refuge in his room after emotional outbursts, usually claiming we were unfair. His dad finally decided something specific must be bothering Benjie, and he set out to discover what it was. And he succeeded. Benjie unloaded his heavy secret: For some months, the fifth-grade boys had been proving their courage to each other by lifting small items from the store during lunch hour.

Dad reacted quietly and firmly; he and Benjie compiled a

list of everything Benjie could remember taking, and they went together to talk to the store manager. Benjie told his story with difficulty, and restitution was agreed upon; the money he earned doing yard work in the neighborhood would be used to pay his debt. He returned home from that encounter a changed boy, subdued and chastened, but freed of a terrible burden.

A child has a basic need for correction. If parents choose to ignore a misdemeanor, the child is confused. He knows he is guilty and wants that guilt to be removed. All children will deny it, but deep inside they want someone to help them do what they know is right and to follow through with fitting consequences when they do what is wrong. Correction gives them security.

ESTABLISH REASONABLE RULES

"How do I get my kids to mind? Why are they so irresponsible? I tell them something one minute, and the next minute I have to turn around and tell them again. What's wrong with them?"

If this person sounds like you, perhaps you need to find the source of your problem. Could you be asking the impossible of your children with overly rigid rules and regulations? Are your rules unclear and subject to rapid change?

Establishing rules requires thoughtful care and sensitivity—and should include much input from your children, too. Once you set a rule, your child is only responsible to obey it or suffer the consequences; *you* are responsible to see it through. So be very careful how you give orders! Give only reasonable and necessary ones. They make life simpler for parents and children alike.

The ice cream man came through our neighborhood every weekday afternoon. His jangling bells sent children running home for change. It was a problem with our four youngsters who wanted to buy ice cream on a continual basis, until we reached a firm agreement: ice cream bars only on Tuesday and Friday. On any other day there was no point in asking. That rule ended a point of frustration for us all.

Among the boundaries that must be set are household rules—what is allowed and not allowed in your home. A household rule we've found to be especially helpful deals with how quickly you expect your children to obey—when you've spoken once? Twice? Parents who ask, "How do I get my kids to mind?" have probably not agreed together on that point. As a result, their children may have learned to ignore their parents' voice until it is raised to final-warning pitch. Firmness, consistency, and clarity are necessary for orderly family life.

Keep your rules simple, and make sure your child understands clearly what is expected of him. A teacher shared her approach with us.

I have found an effective method of dealing with behavior problems. I write down the misbehavior, what I expect the student to do about it, and what I will have to do if the child does not fulfill that expectation. I talk it over with the student, making sure he understands. By putting it in writing, I avoid the easy excuses of "I didn't hear you" or "I forgot."

APPLY CAREFUL CORRECTION

Although we can minimize the need for correction by providing support and guidance, endeavoring to meet basic needs, and establishing reasonable rules, we won't be able to eliminate correction altogether. As Billy Graham so aptly puts it, "Children don't have to be taught to misbehave; it comes naturally."

Once your child has flouted the rules, how can you administer correction without tearing down his self-esteem?

First, check your attitude. If you are steaming with anger,

you're probably not in control. At this point, your correction will serve no further purpose than helping you to release some of your steam. The love and forgiveness so necessary for correction will not be present if anger is the force behind your action.

When anger takes charge of your behavior, your natural tendency will be to verbally attack your child. The effects of your attack will only be negative, though. You will hurt your child's self-worth as well as his respect for you. His behavior may change, but only superficially, to escape the crisis of the moment.

If you do lash out in anger at your child, as every parent will sometimes do, ask your child's forgiveness for your attitude. But make it clear that some form of correction was necessary as a consequence of his behavior.

Second, let your child know which behavior was wrong. When he is corrected for what he thought was all right, or for what he got away with yesterday (and this happens in every home), he becomes confused. He won't see any need to change his behavior.

Third, consider what type of correction is appropriate. Thunder and lightning are hardly necessary for two uneaten prunes! If the misdemeanor is just childish irresponsibility, natural or logical consequences are in order. If outright defiance is involved, an inflicted consequence is more appropriate.

NATURAL CONSEQUENCES

Many times, allowing a child to experience the natural consequences of a mistake is a good corrective measure. It might mean he loses a favorite toy that was ruined because he left it out in the rain. Or it might mean he will get along without a bike for a while if his was stolen because he didn't put it away in the garage (if that is a household rule). A natural consequence is one that usually occurs naturally as a result of the misbehavior and does not need to be planned.

LOGICAL CONSEQUENCES

If a natural consequence of childish irresponsibility would be dangerous or otherwise inappropriate, use a correction related to the offense. A child who has picked the neighbor's flowers may need to be taken by the hand to go apologize to the neighbor. Little Sister may have to do extra jobs to pay for the repair or replacement of a necklace she broke while she was off-limits in Big Sister's room. If you find Billy sitting in front of the TV when he has been told to do his homework first, try restricting his use of the TV.

When I was growing up, the coat closet was in a corner of the living room. We were instructed to close the closet door so that its normal family disarray could not be viewed by anyone coming to the front door. If we ignored that rule, we had to walk across the room and close the door (without slamming it), then retrace our steps and repeat the process three times.

A similar correction was just as effective when, after I had stamped angrily up the stairs, I was made to come back down and go up again quietly—three times! In both instances, the correction worked, and sometimes Mother and I were laughing together by the time I'd made the third round.

Childish irresponsibility almost always calls for just such a simple, logical consequence.

INFLICTED CONSEQUENCES

If a child is extremely willful and deliberately disobeys his parents, another form of consequence may be required. Dr. James Dobson, a recognized child authority, recommends the old-fashioned spanking.

No other form of discipline is as effective as a spanking when willful defiance is involved. . . . Corporal punishment is not a "last resort" to be applied after you have screamed, yelled,

*cried, begged, deprived, wept, and stood him in the corner. It is
to be used any time he chooses to stiffen his neck, clench his
fists, and toss his little pinkie across the line you've drawn in
the dirt.*[6]

But don't spank your child when you are angry. Before
the spanking, calmly explain why you consider it necessary.
Afterward, hold and comfort him, making sure he feels
reassured of your love.

By the third or fourth year of school, and much earlier for
some children, the deprivation of a privilege is an effective
disciplinary tool. With older teenagers, use of the family car
is a marvelous motivator!

For some children, a scolding can be an adequate inflicted
consequence. The knowledge of his parents' disapproval can
be as painful as physical punishment to a sensitive child,
necessitating extra reaffirmation from parents afterward.
Selecting the appropriate consequence comes back to
knowing your child!

Whatever form of correction parents choose, they should
exercise it in private. Public correction, even if it is only a
verbal reprimand, will just trigger a child's defense
mechanisms. For parents, private correction gives the
opportunity for a cool-down period as well as the assurance
of face-to-face communication with their child. It lessens
their likelihood of performing—chastening the child for the
benefit of observers.

In addition, private correction is more likely to make a
lasting impression on a child than public correction. Correc-
tion in front of brothers and sisters may fuel the fires of
sibling rivalry; correction in front of peers may lead to
playground taunts and the ensuing loss of self-esteem.
Either way, the child is distracted from the lesson at hand
by his concern about the reactions of others. He may feel
too humiliated and angry to receive your love and forgive-
ness when it's all over.

I was told to correct my children on the spot, no matter where we were, and never to express love when I was giving correction because it would confuse them. How I regret following that well-intentioned advice.

Reassuring your child of your unchanging, anyhow *love is an essential part of the discipline process.* When your child reaches the teen years, it will be even more important that you show you accept him, even if you reject his behavior. Remember, you do not have a problem child, you have a child with a problem.

WHEN DISCIPLINE DOESN'T WORK

Our prescription for preventive care is not infallible. All parents of grown children have some regrets, regardless of how carefully they disciplined.

Some parents feel like failures. Others feel desperation. These emotions are especially and tragically strong when a willful child's rebellion continues into the older teen years and beyond, when the prodigal son or daughter remains in the far country. The grief of the parents is compounded by the demands our society makes on them.

[Parents] are supposed to be 100 percent adequate, and it is a terrible disgrace if they are not. If they are successful, their children will reward them with devoted love, obedience, and success; if they are not, their children will turn out to be unloving, disobedient, and unsuccessful. This is the prevailing conviction of our society. But when parents buy this notion, they put themselves in an impossible position.[7]

In the Christian community, one is apt to hear some painfully judgmental attitudes: "If children go wrong, it's because they haven't been brought up in the nurture and admonition of the Lord. If you nurture the seedling properly, the tree will grow strong." How much false guilt is heaped on us as parents! One mother tells a familiar story:

We did everything we could, by precept and example, to teach our boy the right way. Our marriage was strong. We played and prayed together with our son, and we enjoyed each other. Our home was happy. According to the books we provided an ideal environment for emotional stability and Christian growth, and our son made a profession of faith as a young boy.

But we could not control all the influences in his life. After some difficult, rebellious years, and despite much counseling from pastors and professionals, our son left us and went the way of the world, his life more or less controlled by alcohol.

Our grief was intensified by the sense that we must be the ones to blame. All our lives we had heard, "Train up a child in the way he should go: and when he is old, he will not depart from it" (Prov. 22:6, KJV). We have been overwhelmed and tormented by feelings of guilt, having failed in the greatest task we have ever undertaken.

No, the prescription is not infallible. Sometimes our best isn't enough. As this mother discovered, there are powerful forces at work in this world, influences sometimes beyond our control (Eph. 6:12; 1 Pet. 5:8). But Christians can cling to the truth that while these influences may separate a beloved child from fellowship with God, they cannot separate him from the love of God (Rom. 8:38-39).

If your child is rebelling against you and God, you need to accept that he is responsible for his own life. You have done the best you could do in the light of your weaknesses and limitations. Now you must leave him and his future in God's hands.

THE END RESULT OF DISCIPLINE

Ideally, discipline leads to discipling, a preparation for following God. Jesus discipled by total involvement in the lives of twelve men. He did not merely live with them, he lived before them with the purpose of making them into God's ambassadors. He prepared them to carry on where he left off.

Jesus' training occurred by the example of his life as much as by his words. Through his own obedience to the Father, he taught his disciples to obey. Through his sacrificial prayer life, he taught them to depend on God. He taught principles naturally, through little incidents that occurred along the way, but he also taught through discourse when the time was right and his followers were ready to listen.

In each of these ways, we can follow Jesus' pattern as we disciple our children. Our calling as parents requires more than just living in the same house as our children and keeping enough order to survive. It requires involvement in their lives with the purpose of training them to be God's disciples.

Perhaps one of the best ways you can achieve this purpose is to relax and enjoy life with your children. Take time to run outside and look at the caterpillar or see the elephant in the clouds. Share the wonder and excitement they feel. Let them know that you, too, treasure those moments. George Will has written:

It is principally by the quality of their attentiveness that parents help children achieve serenity and self-esteem. . . . All children have a sweet tooth for praise, and there is no praise as sweet as being taken seriously, for example, by a parent who reads to you.[8]

There *are* things more important in life than a clean house and a tight schedule, and taking your children seriously is one of them. Remember, "Only dull people have immaculate houses." Don't let your little ones find you dull and preoccupied! Your attitude can make life exciting for them. Children delight in spontaneity and playfulness. We dare not let precious moments slip through our fingers, never to be regained, in the name of schedule.

Self-esteem is more caught than taught. In all of your interaction with your children, you are disciplining them and teaching them. Be careful to build godly values and healthy self-concept. Prepare them for the time when your leadership is over and they are on their own in their walk with God.

Many young people leave the nest with an attitude of, "At last I'm free! No one is going to tell me what to do anymore!" But if you are committed to your own walk with God, and to his parenting example, you will help your child make a smooth transition from your discipleship to God's.

That's the end result of discipline—healthy self-esteem through godly discipling.

QUESTIONS FOR PERSONAL APPLICATION

1. What is the first thought that comes to your mind when you think of the word *discipline?*
2. Can you think of specific times when you *punished* your children, according to the definition on page 198? When you *disciplined* them? What was your attitude in each instance? What were the obvious results in the child? What may have been some unseen results?
3. Which of the four types of parenting best describes the parenting you received? Which type best describes you? When and why do you fall into the undesirable styles of parenting?
4. How might it be possible for a Christian to exhibit the fruit of the Spirit when disciplining children?
5. Which of the marks of an authoritative parent do you most consistently exhibit? Which two do you most need to improve? What specific changes will you begin to make today?
6. How can you gain a child's respect?
7. Can you recall specific instances when you could have met a basic need with patience and understanding rather than with correction? What could you specifically do the next time such needs arise? Which type of correction would be most appropriate?
8. What rules are needed in your home right now? Plan a time to discuss them with your mate. Make a date for a family fun and forum night to implement the new house rules.
9. How many times do you tell your children what you want them to do before following through with correction? What tone of voice gets action? Do you need to make a change in your methods of correction?

10. What are some examples of natural consequences that might occur when one of your house rules is broken? What logical consequences could you begin to use for childish irresponsibility? When might you need to use an inflicted consequence other than spanking? What would be effective in curbing willful defiance?
11. Plan exactly what you will do the next time inflicted consequences are necessary.
12. What are some of your goals for your children? Which would you list as the most important?

QUESTIONS FOR GROUP DISCUSSION

1. Why does punishment result in the negative reactions listed on page 198? Why does discipline elicit positive reactions?
2. Explain the difference between authoritarian and authoritative. Which do you think is the most effective approach to child-rearing? Why?
3. Why might children of authoritarian and neglectful parents want to identify with a counterculture?
4. List some of the lifetime benefits to the person who learns self-control in his childhood.
5. Consider the quote by A. W. Tozer on page 200. Do you agree that "goodness without justice is not goodness"? Why or why not?
6. Do you think it is possible for a Christian to exhibit the fruits of the Spirit when disciplining his children? How?
7. Which characteristics of an authoritative parent are most important? Why?
8. Discuss question 6 from Questions for Personal Application.
9. Share with the group rules that have alleviated some of the need for correction in your home.
10. Why do you need to be careful how you give orders?
11. Discuss question 10 from Questions for Personal Application.
12. How could you explain to a willful child and a sensitive child why you discipline them differently?

Conclusion
Spread the Cure

Just as there is no perfect parent on the face of the earth, so there are no perfect relationships. Nor is there perfect happiness or perfect godliness in this life. We all fail to understand God's acceptance. We all fail in passing that acceptance on to others. We will never achieve perfectly healthy self-esteem.

God's people tend to suffer a lot of false guilt over sins they have already confessed and received forgiveness for. The big ones and the minor ones. Even attitudes. We long to live lives that are beyond reproach. We want to be perfect parents, perfect children, perfect friends, perfect Christians, perfect people. But we are not always empathetic and forgiving. We have trouble demonstrating unconditional love. We are not always kind. Sometimes we even have temper tantrums. And sometimes we are blanketed by depression.

Why do we have all the struggle? Why is it so difficult to see ourselves as God sees us—on the one hand, sinners who cannot be good enough to please him; on the other hand, his beloved children, forgiven and restored? One reason, as we've discovered, is that we're often preoccupied with the opinions of other people rather than with God's. We've adopted this world's standards. We judge ourselves and others by those standards, forgetting all that the Father has to say about us.

But as we begin to recognize and accept our standing in *God's* value system, we can be free from the struggle for self-esteem, the maneuvers to bolster our egos, the fight for our place in the pecking order. Freedom will come when our views of ourselves don't depend on the looks, physique, or intelligence we inherited, the family we were born into, the size of our bank account, or even how others treat us. A general principle is: When you feel comfortable about yourself, about who you are and what you have, you can direct your focus away from yourself and toward others.

If we could just get a mind-set on eternal values! Our chief purpose in life is not to protect and promote ourselves but to glorify the Father. That purpose is shared by every Christian and every Christian home. But how can we worship God if we're focused on ourselves?

A healthy, outward-focused self-esteem will not only enhance our relationship with God but also will help us keep other people in proper perspective. Put others first and follow the mandate of Scripture: "Do not merely look out for your own personal interests, but also for the interests of others" (Phil. 2:4, NASB). When we recognize that *everything we are and have comes from him,* our self-esteem will stabilize, and God's love can flow through us to others. Perhaps that is the beginning and the end of our worship.

Unfortunately, the Christian home is in battle with Satan, just as the individual believer is. The enemy will use any device for dividing us, for destroying our peace, for breaking down our communication, for leading us away from God. When he defeats us personally in any way—through anger, depression, self-pity, or simply a negative self-image—he gets his foot in the door of our homes. We are in spiritual battle every day of our lives; we must recognize it for what it is!

We must be armed. We must know what God has to say about us. Equipped with that knowledge, protection, and strength, we won't need to fall victim to Satan's assaults on our self-esteem, designed to perpetuate our self-focus. We no longer need to feel unloved or unworthy or inadequate. We can be healthy emotionally as well as spiritually.

God loves you, just as you are, with an everlasting love. Do you accept that fact? Do you believe him?

Perhaps your biggest problem is that you have been focusing on what people think of you (or what you think they think of you). But Christ does not reject you. Christ has never mocked you or laughed at you. Keeping that fact in mind, you *can* conquer a negative self-image. By deliberately de-emphasizing the world's values and dwelling on the values of Christ, you can develop healthy, biblical self-esteem—and reach out to build it in others. You, too, can share God's *anyhow* love, his total, unconditional acceptance.

That's how healthy people spread the cure.

QUESTIONS FOR PERSONAL
APPLICATION AND GROUP DISCUSSION

1. Why is an adequate self-concept a prerequisite to successful living?
2. How would the knowledge that everything you are or have comes from God affect your self-image?
3. What are God's values?
4. List some practical steps you can take to set your mind on eternal values.
5. How can you defeat Satan when you sense he is attacking you or your home through anger, depression, self-pity, or pride? (See James 4:7-8; Eph. 1:19-23; 4:27; 6:11-18; 1 Pet. 5:6-10; 1 John 4:4.)
6. What do you consider the most important outcome of developing healthy self-esteem?
7. In what ways can a person who knows Christ build up others?

Appendix
Ten Steps to Healthy Self-Esteem

1. Tell the truth about God, yourself, and others.
2. Remember that everyone suffers with unhealthy self-esteem to some degree, so you don't need to be afraid to reach out with love, acceptance, and reassurance. Others need this from you. They will benefit—and so will you!
3. Get to the root of any lingering "I'm no good" feelings by evaluating all the facets of your self-image and trying to remember the possible causes of your negative attitudes.
4. Understand that your self-worth has been determined largely by the world's temporal, fickle values and by faulty communication:
   a. Your interpretation of messages hasn't always matched the sender's intent.
   b. Most of your interaction has been with others who need to build up their own low self-esteem, regardless of the cost to yours.
5. Check to see if some facets of your self-image need improvement. Be honest now! You do have to live in this world, whether or not you agree with all its standards.

6. Ask God to help you replace your negative self-concept with positive self-assurance based on his values.

7. Thank God for using your weaknesses to draw you to him. It is those weaknesses that force you to lean on him. If your life were perfect, you wouldn't see your need for him.

8. If your poor self-esteem stems from guilt, confess it, claim God's promise of forgiveness, and apply Romans 8:28: "And we know that in all things God works for the good of those who love him, who have been called according to his purpose" (NIV).

9. Begin to focus on God's values by:
   a. Thanking him every day for what he has done for you and for his high estimation of you.
   b. Searching the Scriptures to find items to put in a "praise" list.

10. Concentrate on others' needs by planning ways to help them appreciate who and what they are.

FOOTNOTES

CHAPTER ONE
[1]C. S. Lewis, *The Screwtape Letters* (New York: Macmillan, 1954), 72-73.
[2]C. S. Lewis, *Mere Christianity* (New York: Macmillan, 1942), 99.

CHAPTER THREE
[1]William D. Brooks and Philip Emmert, *Interpersonal Communication* (Dubuque, Iowa: William C. Brown Co., 1976), 44.
[2]Yvonne Dunleavy, "Why We Do Those Dumb Little Things?" *Ladies' Home Journal* (November 1982), 52. Reprinted with permission of the author and *Ladies' Home Journal,* copyright 1982 by Family Media, Inc.
[3]Ibid.

CHAPTER FOUR
[1]Gregg Lewis, "All the Homely People," *Campus Life* (February 1979), 61.
[2]Dr. James Dobson, *Hide or Seek* (Old Tappan, N.J.: Fleming H. Revell, 1974, 1979), 24-25. Used by permission.
[3]Lewis, 63.
[4]Moses Chase, "Ugly Clear to the Bone," *Moody Monthly* (July/August 1976), 91.
[5]Lewis, 63.
[6]Ibid.

CHAPTER FIVE
[1]S. Rickly Christian, "The Big Ten," *Campus Life* (February 1981), 43.
[2]Dr. James Dobson, *Hide or Seek* (Old Tappan, N.J.: Fleming H. Revell, 1974, 1979), 51-52. Used by permission.

[3]Nathaniel Sheppard, Jr., New York Times Service, *The Cedar Rapids Gazette* (April 1981).

[4]Ibid.

[5]S. Rickly Christian, "Joyfully Crazed," *Campus Life* (November 1980), 40.

CHAPTER SIX

[1]Paul Lee Tan, *Encyclopedia of 7700 Illustrations: Signs of the Times* (Rockville, Md.: Assurance, 1979), 824.

[2]Grace Hechinger, "Happy Mother's Day," *Newsweek* (May 11, 1981), 19.

CHAPTER SEVEN

[1]Herbert Vander Lugt, *Our Daily Bread* (June 12, 1981).

[2]Richard Hunter, "Behold the Preacher," *A.D. Magazine* (1980).

CHAPTER TEN

[1]Dr. James Dobson, *Hide or Seek* (Old Tappan, N.J.: Fleming H. Revell, 1974, 1979), 151-165. Used by permission.

[2]Gene Seligmann with Eric Gelman, "A Schlemiel Syndrome," *Newsweek* (September 15, 1980).

[3]Fran Carpentier, "Everybody Loves a Loser," *Parade* (March 16, 1980).

[4]Gene Shalit, "What's Happening?" *Ladies' Home Journal* (February 1980), 30. Used by permission of the author and *Ladies' Home Journal,* copyright 1980 by Meredith Publications, Inc.

[5]Dobson, *Hide or Seek,* 154.

[6]David Gelman, et al., "The Games Teenagers Play," *Newsweek* (September 1, 1980), 48.

[7]Abigail Van Buren, "Dear Abby" (Universal Press Syndicate, 1980).

CHAPTER ELEVEN

[1]Dr. David Stoop, *Self-Talk: Key to Personal Growth* (Old Tappan, N.J.: Fleming H. Revell, 1982), 65-67. Used by permission.

[2]Ibid., 75.

[3]David Augsburger, *The Freedom of Forgiveness* (Chicago: Moody Press, 1970), 34-35. Used by permission.

[4]Ibid., 33, 37.

[5]William Backus and Marie Chapian, *Telling Yourself the Truth* (Minneapolis, Minn.: Bethany House, 1980), 15, 17.

CHAPTER TWELVE

[1]Norman Wakefield, *Building Self-Esteem in the Family* (Elgin, Ill.: David C. Cook, 1977). Used with permission.

[2]Waylon Ward, "Who Does Your Child Think He Is?" *Moody Monthly* (January 1980), 104.

[3]Wakefield.

[4]Albert Mehabriar, *Silent Messages* (Belmont, Calif.: Wadsworth Publishing, 1971), 42-44. Used with permission.

[5]Ward, 104.
[6]Wakefield.
[7]Henry T. Close, "On Parenting," *VOICES: The Art and Science of Psychotherapy,* vol. 4, no. 1 (Spring 1968).

CHAPTER THIRTEEN
[1]Norman Wakefield, *Building Self-Esteem in the Family* (Elgin, Ill.: David C. Cook, 1977). Used with permission.
[2]Dr. James Dobson, *Hide or Seek* (Old Tappan, N.J.: Fleming H. Revell, 1974, 1979), 60.
[3]Ray Noel, "Family Happiness Is Homemade," *Family Concern* (October 1980).
[4]H. Norman Wright, *Improving Your Self-Image* (Eugene, Oreg.: Harvest House, 1977), 29. Used by permission.
[5]Mary Alice Loberg, *A Friend Indeed* (Kansas City: Hallmark, 1971).

CHAPTER FOURTEEN
[1]Norman Wakefield, *Building Self-Esteem in the Family* (Elgin, Ill.: David C. Cook, 1977). Used with permission.
[2]Dr. Neil Solomon, Los Angeles Times Syndicate, *The Cedar Rapids Gazette* (April 5, 1981).
[3]Dr. James Dobson, *Hide or Seek* (Old Tappan, N.J.: Fleming H. Revell, 1974, 1979), 101.
[4]Catherine McKenzie, "Emotional Abuse Debilitates Child," *The Cedar Rapids Gazette* (June 28, 1981).

CHAPTER FIFTEEN
[1]"The Little Boy and the Old Man," in *A Light in the Attic: The Poems and Drawings of Shel Silverstein* (New York: Harper & Row, 1981). Used by permission.

CHAPTER SIXTEEN
[1]Henry R. Brandt and Homer E. Dowdy, *Building a Christian Home* (Wheaton, Ill.: Scripture Press, 1960), 104.
[2]Andrew Wigert, Darwin Thomas, and Viktor Gecas, *Family and Socialization: A Quest for Theory* (Portland, Oreg.: National Council of Family Relations, 1972), 3ff.
[3]Ibid.
[4]A. W. Tozer, *The Knowledge of the Holy* (New York: Harper & Row, 1961), 85, 94.
[5]Joy Wilt, *Happily Ever After* (Waco, Tex.: Word, 1977), 101.
[6]Dr. James Dobson, *Hide or Seek* (Old Tappan, N.J.: Fleming H. Revell, 1974, 1979), 93-94.
[7]Henry T. Close, "On Parenting," *VOICES: The Art and Science of Psychotherapy,* vol. 4, no. 1 (Spring 1968).
[8]George Will, *The Orlando Sentinel* (November 12, 1981).